ANIMAL WATCH

A Visual Introduction to

MONKEYS
AND APES

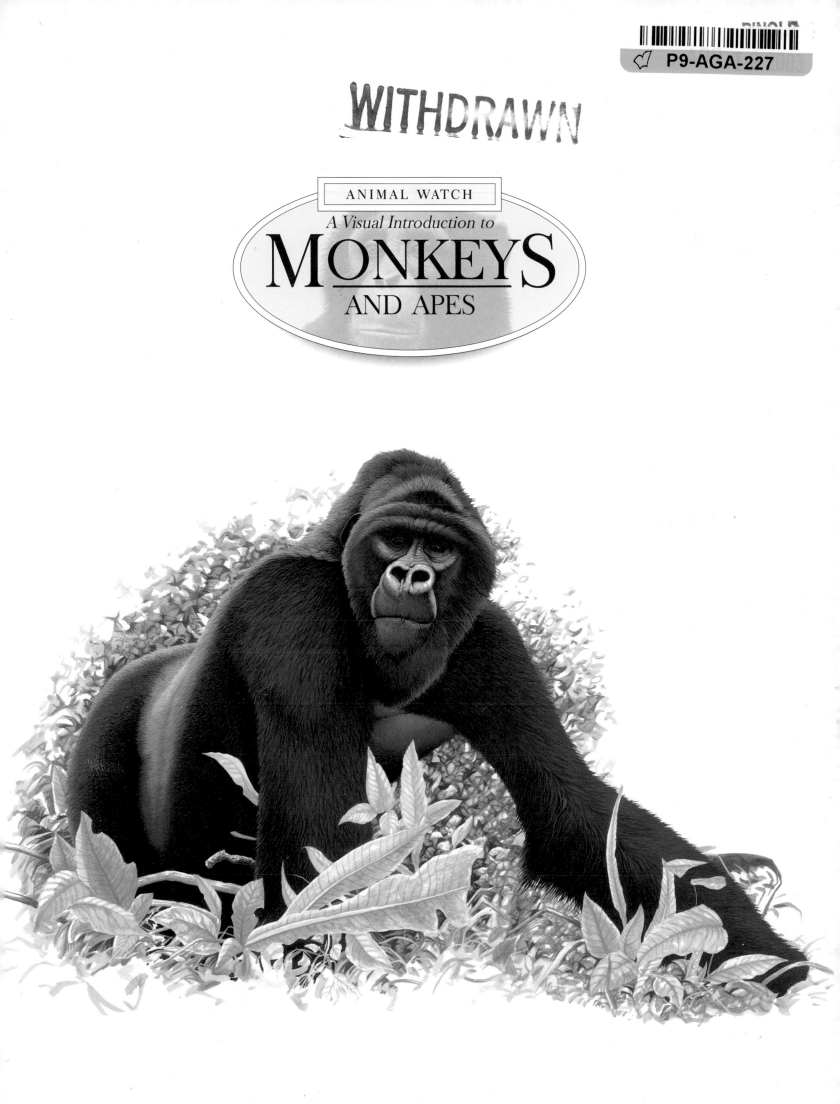

A Visual Introduction to Monkeys and Apes
Copyright © 2000 AND Cartographic Publishers Ltd
http://www.and.nl
Created and Packaged by Firecrest Books Ltd. in association
with AND Cartographic Publishers Ltd.

Checkmark Books
An imprint of Facts On File, Inc.
11 Penn Plaza
New York NY 10001

Library of Congress Cataloging-in-Publication Data
Stonehouse, Bernard.
Monkeys and apes: A visual introduction to monkeys and apes/
Bernard Stonehouse:
illustrated by Richard Orr.
New York : Checkmark Books, 1999
p. cm. — Animal watch QL737.P9S759 1999
599.8.21
Introduces the physical characteristics, behavior, and habitats of
primates, including lemurs, monkeys, apes and humans.
ISBN 0-8160-3927-5
1. Primates — Juvenile literature. [1. Primates] I. Orr, Richard,
ill. II. Title. III. Series: Stonehouse, Bernard. Animal Watch.
99-23828

Checkmark Books are available at special discounts when
purchased in bulk quantities for businesses, associations,
institutions or sales promotions. Please call our Special Sales
Department in New York at (212) 967-8800 or (800) 322-8755.

You can find Facts On File on the World Wide Web at
http://www.factsonfile.com

ANIMAL WATCH

A Visual Introduction to

MONKEYS

AND APES

Bernard Stonehouse

☑®

Checkmark Books™

An imprint of Facts On File, Inc.

PICTURE CREDITS

Pages 8-9: Oxford Scientific Films

Pages 10-11 : Still Pictures

Pages 12-13: Planet Earth; Woodfall Wild Images; Still Pictures

Pages 14-15: BBC Natural History Unit Picture Library; Planet Earth

Pages 16-17: Natural History Photographic Agency;
Oxford Scientific Films

Pages 18-19: BBC Natural History Unit Picture Library;
Oxford Scientific Films; Frank Lane Picture Agency

Pages 20-21: Natural History Photographic Agency; Still Pictures

Pages 22-23: Planet Earth; BBC Natural History Unit Picture Library

Pages 24-25: Planet Earth; Frank Lane Picture Agency;
Natural History Photographic Agency

Pages 26-27: Woodfall Wild Images; BBC Natural History Unit
Picture Library

Pages 28-29: BBC Natural History Unit Picture Library

Pages 30-31: BBC Natural History Unit Picture Library; Still Pictures;
Natural History Photographic Agency

Pages 32-33: BBC Natural History Unit Picture Library; Planet Earth

Pages 34-35: Still Pictures; BBC Natural History Unit Picture Library

Pages 36-37: Frank Lane Picture Agency

Pages 38-39: Still Pictures; Oxford Scientific Films;
Frank Lane Picture Agency

Pages 40-41: Natural History Photographic Agency;
Topham Picturepoint

Pages 42-43: Woodfall Wild Images; Oxford Scientific Films

All satellite mapping: WorldSat

Artwork by

Richard Orr/Bernard Thornton Artists Cover, pp14-25, 28-29

Martin Camm pp8-9, 12-13, 32-33, 36-39

Lucia Guarnotta pp10-11, 30-31, 42-43

Gabriele Maschietti pp24 (talapoin), 26-27

Art and editorial direction by **Peter Sackett**

Edited by **Norman Barrett**

Designed by **Paul Richards, Designers & Partners**

Picture research by **Lis Sackett**

Printed in **China**

CONTENTS

PRIMATES

Monkeys, apes and humans are all included in a natural group of mammals called the Primates (the correct pronunciation is Pry-*may*-tees, but most people just say "**pry**-mates"). Mammals are warm-blooded animals that feed their young on milk. Biologists divide them into about 20 different groups, or "orders." Other orders of mammals include Cetacea (whales and dolphins), Carnivora (cats, dogs and other meateaters), Rodentia (rats, mice, squirrels), Pinnipedia (seals and walruses), Insectivora (hedgehogs and shrews) and Chiroptera (bats).

Carolus Linnaeus, a Swedish biologist who lived in the 1700s, was the first to classify animals into natural groupings. He regarded humans as the highest of all creatures, so he put them into the order called "Primates," meaning "first." When he saw that monkeys and apes were in many ways similar to humans, he classified them as primates too. Then three other groups of mammals, the lemurs, lorises and tarsiers, were found to be similar to monkeys, and included as well.

RELATIONSHIPS

In grouping animals together, Linnaeus was not suggesting that they were closely related. He implied only that they were similar in ways that seemed important. Ideas that animals within groups are closely related, and must have "evolved" from common ancestors, came later (see page 41).

INTRODUCING THE PRIMATES

The animals closest to humans.

MONKEYS AND APES are our closest relatives in the animal kingdom. Together with humans, they make up a group in the order of Primates. The "family tree" below shows how we think the different groups within the Primates may be related to each other.

On the left are some representatives of the Prosimii (see "Three Groups" in the box below). This suborder contains over 30 living species (different kinds) of animals, mostly cat-sized or smaller. Lemurs and their kin live only in the forests of some islands off the east coast of Africa. Lorises and bush babies live in Africa and southern Asia. In the middle are the Tarsoidea, a much smaller group of only three or four living species. About as big as rats or young rabbits, these too live in trees, in some of the island forests of southeastern Asia.

On the right is a selection of the Anthropoidea, the main suborder of Primates.

LEMURS AND LORISES

TARSIERS

NEW WORLD MONKEYS

OLD WORLD MONKEYS

ANCESTRAL PRIMATE

THREE GROUPS

Today we divide the order Primates into three suborders:

■ Prosimii (Pro-*sim*-ee-i), or prosimians, containing the lemurs and lorises
■ Tarsioidea (**Tarsi**-o-**id**-ea), containing only the tarsiers, which are very similar to prosimians, less so to monkeys and apes
■ Anthropoidea (**An**-thro-po-**id**-ea), containing monkeys, apes and humans

This book is mainly about the Anthropoidea, but you will meet some of the lemurs, lorises and tarsiers on pages 10–11.

TODAYS PRIMATES

Lemurs and lorises

Tarsiers

Apes and monkeys

WHAT MAKES

Though lorises, monkeys, apes and humans are at first sight very different, they have several important features in common—important enough for them all to be included in the Primates:

■ They walk on flat feet, not on their toes like cats and dogs, and their feet have padded soles
■ Their toes and fingers mostly have flat nails, not claws
■ The thumbs (often the big toes, too) are separate, so that they can grasp and hold branches
■ The two bones that make up the lower arm and leg are separate, so the hands and feet can twist and turn

Where do they live?

This is a much bigger group, containing 138 living species—127 species of monkeys, 10 species of apes and just one species of humans. Most of the monkeys are small, living in trees among or close to forests, mainly in tropical and temperate regions. Apes tend to be larger. They live in trees, too, and also on the ground, in warm forested country. Stocks of humanlike apes arose from apelike ancestors and spread from the forests to open plains and coasts. Humans, whether or not they evolved from these creatures (see page 40), spread to every part of the world.

APES

Note: The weights and other measurements given in this book, unless otherwise indicated, are for an average adult male

A PRIMATE?

- They have a large brain, and a large, rounded skull to contain it
- The eyes look forward rather than sideways
- The milk glands are on the chest, not on the abdomen
- They grow slowly, staying longer than most other mammals in the care of their parents

These are the important similarities. The differences will become apparent as you move from one group to another through the book.

WHERE DID MONKEYS AND APES COME FROM?

Millions of years ago the world's continents existed as one great landmass, across which animals could roam freely. Some 200 million years ago this land mass began to split into the continents we know today, each continent developing its own stocks of reptiles, birds and mammals.

Australia split away before mammals had diversified into the 20 orders we recognize today, so its only native mammals are marsupials. There are no Australian nonhuman primates.

When Madagascar parted from Africa about 50 million years ago, primates such as the prosimians had come into existence, but not the monkeys and apes. Prosimians survived and continued to vary in their own ways in Madagascar.

Tarsier munching a cicada (a type of flying insect)

Elsewhere they came into competition with the new patterns of anthropoid monkeys, and eventually died out.

As North and South America separated from Europe, Africa and Asia, different kinds of monkeys appeared in the "New World" and "Old World" (see page 13), and apes began to inhabit the forests of Africa and Asia.

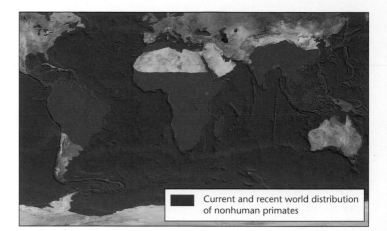

Current and recent world distribution of nonhuman primates

Primates live in most parts of the world, but different groups within the order live more locally. Lemurs and their close kin live only in Madagascar and the nearby Comoro Islands. Lorises and bush babies are found through southern Africa, India, Sri Lanka and southeastern Asia. Tarsiers have a more limited range in Indonesia and the Philippine Islands.

Monkeys are widespread in tropical and temperate forests of Central and South America. In Europe they occur only in Gibraltar, but they range widely across Africa and southern Arabia to India, Sri Lanka and southeastern Asia, then north into China and Japan.

Apes are native to Africa and southeastern Asia. The first humans probably appeared in Africa, but now humans are at home all over the world.

THE FIRST PRIMATES

The first fossils that we recognize as primates appeared in deposits that represent forests of about 100 million years ago. Small animals, about the size of rats, they lived among trees and probably fed on insects. Though we know them only from fossil bones and teeth, we think they must have looked rather like the tree shrews that today live in forests of southeastern Asia. Indeed, some biologists classify the modern tree shrews in the order Primates.

Tree shrew—sometimes classified as a Primate

LEMURS, LORISES AND TARSIERS

Distant cousins of monkeys and apes.

FACT FILE

RING-TAILED LEMUR

Suborder:	Prosimii
Family:	Lemuridae
Scientific name:	*Lemur catta*
Color:	Gray body, white face, black nose and eye rings, black and white striped tail
Weight:	6.6 lb (3 kg)
Length, head and body:	18 in (45 cm)
Habitat:	Forest trees and clearings
Range:	Madagascar

SLENDER LORIS

Suborder:	Prosimii
Family:	Loridae
Scientific name:	*Loris tardigradus*
Color:	Gray-brown body, white face with black eye rings
Weight:	11 oz (300 g)
Length, head and body:	9 in (24 cm)
Habitat:	Forest trees
Range:	Southern India, Sri Lanka

SPECTRAL TARSIER

Suborder:	Tarsioidea
Family:	Tarsiidae
Scientific name:	*Tarsius spectrum*
Color:	Gray body, tufted tail
Weight:	4 oz (110 g)
Length, head and body:	5 in (12 cm)
Habitat:	Forest trees
Range:	Sulawesi (Indonesia)

RELATIONSHIPS

Lemurs and lorises form the suborder Prosimii. The lemur family is made up of 17 species, rather catlike in general appearance, but with long fingers and toes that grasp and wrap around branches. Lorises and their kin the bush babies, smaller than lemurs, form a family of 11 species. Tarsiers are similar, but even tinier, about the size of rats. There are only three living species, which form a suborder, Tarsioidea, of their own.

THESE RING-TAILED LEMURS, sunning themselves in a forest clearing of southwestern Madagascar, form a small mob, or troop, that move around together by day. Lemurs spend much of their time in the trees, climbing and leaping among the branches. Holding on tightly with fingers and toes, they browse on leaves, shoots and fruit. Sharp noses, pointed ears and prominent round eyes give them an inquiring, alert expression. Nearly all have long bushy tails, which they wave in the air as signals to each other.

Lorises are similar but smaller, with rounded ears, large eyes, no tail and slightly worried expressions. The slender loris of Sri Lanka spends its days asleep in a tree, rolled into a ball with head tucked in, and firmly gripping the branches with long fingers and toes. At night it uncurls and patrols slowly among the branches, catching insects and birds, and browsing on fruit, new shoots and leaves. Pottos, bush babies (galagos) and angwantibos are similiar African forms.

Tiny tarsiers, with snub noses and enormous, wondering eyes, have a rather more monkeylike body, with long thin limbs and splayed, padded fingers. They, too, are nocturnal, and almost entirely carnivorous, hunting insects, lizards and birds.

Ring-tailed lemurs

FAMILY LIFE

Ring-tailed lemurs live in groups of a dozen or more adults of both sexes, with perhaps up to a dozen young, which stay together like a large, mobile family. They mate during March and April, and the single young are born about five months later. Within a few minutes of birth the babies are strong enough to hold on to their mothers' fur, and for several weeks they travel piggyback.

Slender lorises live alone, nocturnal and solitary, keeping out of each other's way except during the breeding seasons. Females become ready for mating mainly in November and May, and single cubs are born five to six months later.

Spectral tarsiers live together in pairs, patrolling territories in the forests, often accompanied by one or two young. Most babies are born in November and December, but can appear at any time. Mothers carry them in their mouths for the first two or three weeks. After that they are big enough to keep up with their parents.

Slender loris

Spectral tarsier

Where do they live?

All of these species live in tropical rain forests. Ring-tailed lemurs live in Madagascar, off the southeastern coast of Africa. Other species of lemurs are found only in Madagascar or in the Comoro Islands, farther north in the Indian Ocean. Slender lorises inhabit the forests of southern India and Sri Lanka. Other species of loris, also forest-living, extend from India to Malaysia. Spectral tarsiers live in Sulawesi, east of Borneo, and on forested islands close by. Of the other two species of tarsier, one is found throughout Borneo and Sumatra, the other in the Philippine Islands. Pottos, bush babies and angwantibos live in forests of tropical Africa.

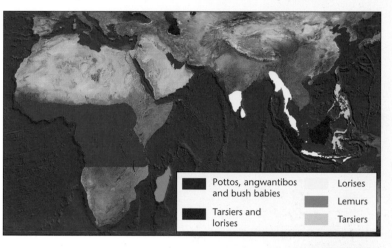

■ Pottos, angwantibos and bush babies	■ Lorises
■ Tarsiers and lorises	■ Lemurs
	■ Tarsiers

SIGHT, HEARING AND SCENT

Like most other primates, prosimians have broad faces with eyes facing forward and slightly outwards. This gives them good forward vision, probably enabling them to judge distances, just as we can. The loris's relatively large eyes, and the huge eyes of tarsiers, help them to see sharply in poor light.

All have relatively large ears, with flaps that can be turned to pick up sounds from different directions.

Less obvious is their acute sense of smell. Most of these animals mark their paths along the forest branches with urine, which others of their own kind recognize. Lemurs

Lemurs looking and listening

especially produce a musky scent from glands on their hands and arms, which probably enables other lemurs to identify them as individuals. By whisking their tails across the glands, they transfer some of the scent to the fur. Waving their tails in the air spreads the scent more widely.

COMBING THE FUR

All mammals have to keep their skin and fur clean, and if possible free from fleas, ticks and other parasites. Most use their claws for scratching, and their tongue for washing and combing. Prosimians have another way—a special comb, made from the front teeth of their lower jaw, to pull through the fur and keep it in good order. Then they push forward a horny plate under the tongue to keep the comb clean.

Red-bellied lemur

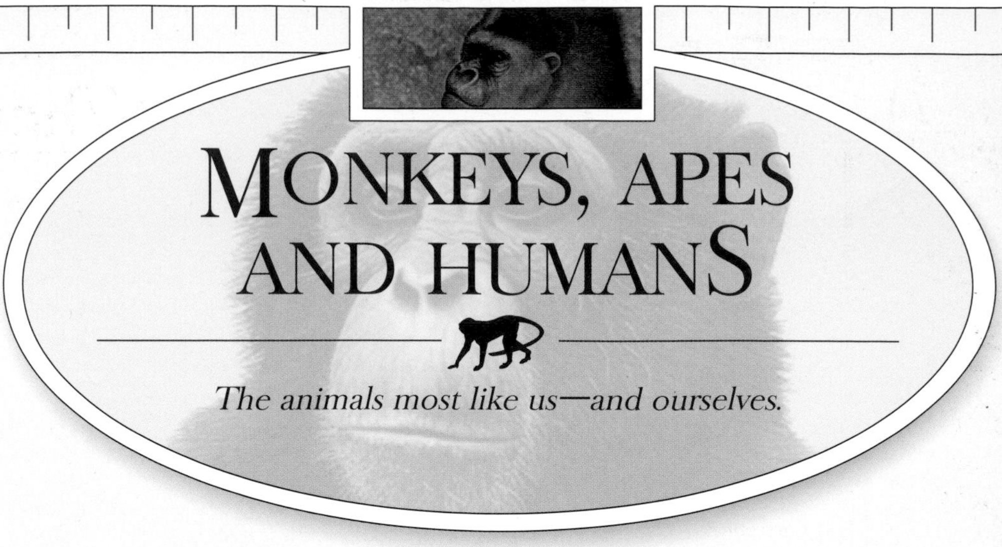

MONKEYS, APES AND HUMANS

The animals most like us—and ourselves.

MONKEYS, APES AND HUMANS are built to very similar plans, with important similarities and differences that reflect their different ways of living.

Monkeys are the smallest, typically about the size of house cats, though some are much smaller and others bigger. They have long limbs, and long fingers and toes. Nearly all live in trees, running and climbing among the branches. A few species, such as the baboons, live mainly on the ground, but can still climb well when they need to. Tree-living monkeys tend to have long, well-muscled hind limbs and relatively short forelimbs. Those that live mainly on the ground have longer arms. Nearly all have tails. The tree-living monkeys have long tails, sometimes longer than the body, which help them to balance. Some South American monkeys have a prehensile (grasping) tail, with a muscular tip that wraps around branches and grasps like an extra hand (see page 17). Ground-living species usually have shorter, stumpy tails or no tail at all. All are vegetarian or omnivorous, eating mainly fruit, buds and leaves, but they take insects and other animals when they can.

Apes are mostly larger and heavier than monkeys, with no tails. One family, the gibbons (see pages 30–31), uses their long arms and legs to swing through the forest canopy. Gorillas, chimpanzees and orangutans, together called the "great apes" (pages 32-39), are less agile. Though all can climb, gorillas and chimpanzees forage mainly on the ground and in the lower branches of the trees, sometimes walking upright, but usually crouching or moving on all four limbs. Orangutans spend more of their lives in the trees.

Humans are similar in size and shape to the great apes, but live almost entirely on the ground. Where the apes are mostly herbivorous, eating leaves and fruit, humans are omnivores, eating vegetation but also hunting other animals. Unlike monkeys and apes, they stand and walk upright, leaving their arms and hands free for other actions and activities. The illustration shows an early form of man, smaller than modern humans, who lived in China, Indonesia, northern Africa and possibly Europe. This species, which used tools and fire, died out about half a million years ago.

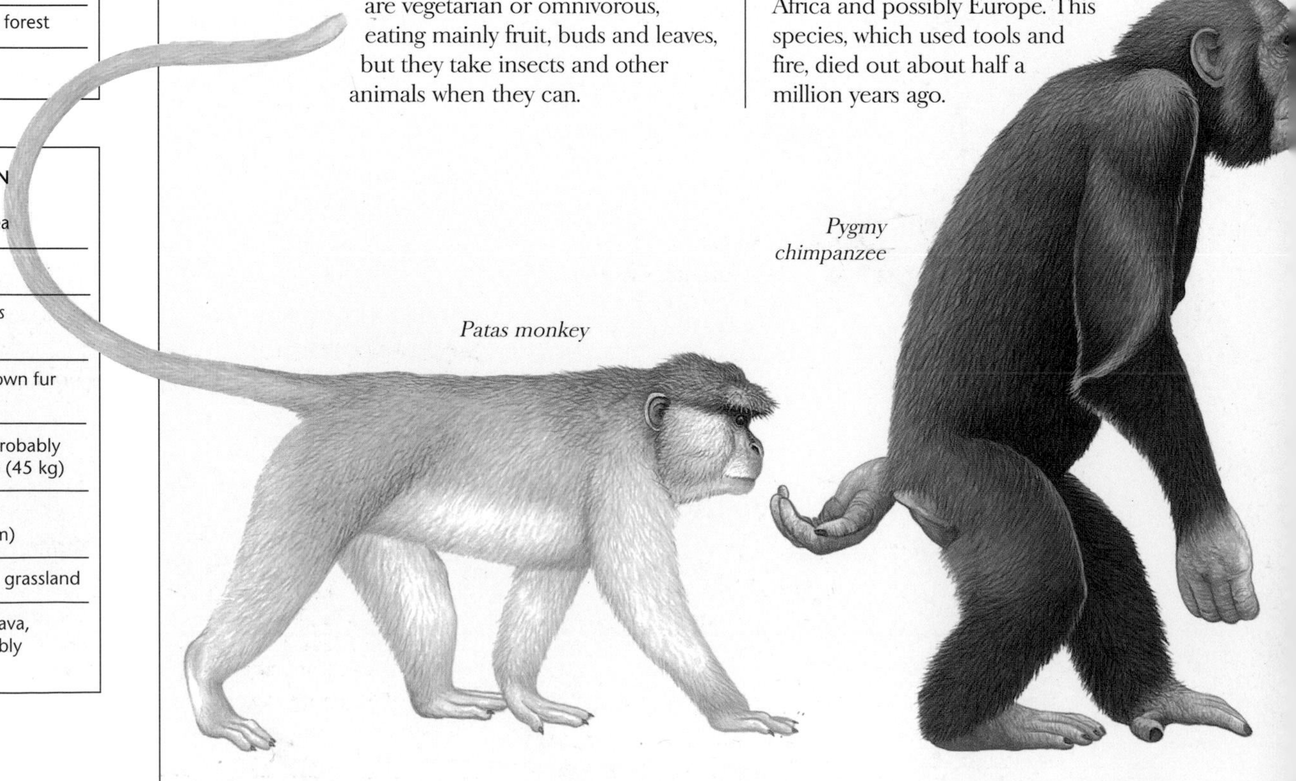

Pygmy chimpanzee

Patas monkey

Patas monkey

Artist's impression of an early human—we do not know what they looked like, but they might have looked something like this

STANDING UPRIGHT

Monkeys often sit up on their haunches, but do not usually stand or walk upright. Apes, including gibbons, can stand upright, and most can walk upright, at least with a crouch, and for a few steps. Only humans stand, walk and run entirely on their hind legs. When danger threatens, monkeys and gibbons swing off through the trees, the great apes race away on all fours, but humans stay upright, striding and running in a way that is all their own.

Pygmy chimpanzee

Lowland gorilla

RELATIONSHIPS

The three primates illustrated (left) are of the more advanced kind—the ones that biologists group in the suborder Anthropoidea (page 8). Patas monkeys are just one of 127 living species of monkeys. You will find out more about them on pages 24–25. Pygmy chimpanzees are one of 10 species of apes (see pages 34–35). Early humans are dealt with more fully on pages 40–41. On these pages we show some of the physical similarities and differences among monkeys, apes and humans.

Where do they live?

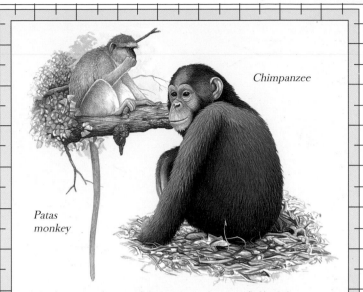

Chimpanzee

Patas monkey

Monkeys spend most of their time in the trees (left) while apes live mostly on the ground (right)

Monkeys generally live in the trees of tropical or subtropical forests, more among the branches than on the ground. Some species—such as the Patas monkeys—feed on open grassland at the forest edge, never straying far from the safety of trees. Patas monkeys are found across central Africa from Senegal in the west to Sudan in the east, and as far south as Tanzania.

Apes, too, live in or near tropical forests. Larger and heavier than monkeys, they spend more of their time on the ground, but still climb trees for food and safety. Pygmy chimpanzees live in the dense rain forests of Congo DR , in central Africa, close to the meeting of the Zaire (Congo) and Lualaba Rivers.

The fossil record tells us that early humans lived in forests and grassland, spent most of their lives on the ground, and walked upright rather than on all fours. The earliest human bones have been found in Africa. From there, humans later spread to Europe, Asia and the rest of the world (see page 41).

OLD WORLD, NEW WORLD

The "Old World" is the continental mass that includes Europe, Asia and Africa. The "New World" is North and South America. When people were emigrating from Europe to North America in the 1800s, they spoke of leaving the old world to find a new life in the new world. The names have stuck, and biologists use the terms when they are describing the different kinds of plant and animal communities on either side of the Atlantic Ocean.

The Old World has 80 species of monkeys, the New World 47 species, but they belong to different families, and none of the species lives in both. Apes occur only in the Old World, some in Africa, others in Asia.

NEW WORLD MONKEYS 1

Marmosets and tamarins—squirrel-like monkeys of the South American forests.

FACT FILE

COMMON MARMOSET

Suborder:	Anthropoidea
Family:	Callitrichidae
Scientific name:	*Callithrix jacchus*
Color:	Variable, gray to dark brown, with pale face and ear tufts
Weight:	12 oz (330 g)
Length, head and body:	8 in (20 cm)
Habitat:	Tropical wet or dry rain forest and savannah
Range:	Southern Amazon river basin, South America

COTTONTOP TAMARIN

Suborder:	Anthropoidea
Family:	Callitrichidae
Scientific name:	*Saguinus oedipus*
Color:	Reddish brown back and hindquarters, white underparts, forelimbs and crest
Weight:	13 oz (360 g)
Length, head and body:	8 in (20 cm)
Habitat:	Tropical rain forest
Range:	Northern Amazon river basin, South America

GOLDEN LION TAMARIN

Suborder:	Anthropoidea
Family:	Callitrichidae
Scientific name:	*Leontopithecus rosalia*
Color:	Golden brown
Weight:	23 oz (650 gm)
Length, head and body:	14 in (35 cm)
Habitat:	Tropical rain forest
Range:	Southern Brazil

MARMOSETS ARE SMALL, fast-moving monkeys, furry and compact, with bushy tails one-and-a-half times as long again as their bodies. Similar in build to the lemurs, and often compared with squirrels, they race up and down the trunks and along the branches of forest trees. If you see one, there are usually several more close at hand. However, they scare easily, and their dull gray and brown fur is good camouflage.

Marmosets feed mainly on insects, spiders and other small animals. They have long, flat front teeth, which they use to scrape gum from tree trunks. Most of their fingers and toes are armed with claws. Only the big toes have flattened nails.

Slightly larger than marmosets, tamarins are more brightly colored, with longer, sleeker fur.

Their canine teeth are long and sharp, like those of a dog or cat. These, too, are lively, squirrel-like animals that forage by day in dense patches of forest. The reddish brown cottontop tamarin gets its name from the prominent tufts of white fur immediately above its eyes. Lion or golden lion tamarins have long yellowish golden fur, with an even longer swept back mane covering the head and shoulders. These are now among the rarest of all monkeys (see page 43).

Cottontop tamarin

Golden lion tamarin

Emperor tamarin

RELATIONSHIPS

The 47 or so species of New World monkeys are listed by some biologists in one family, the Cebidae. Others separate the marmosets and tamarins into a family of their own, the Callitrichidae, and that is how we divide them here. The five species of marmosets and 12 of tamarins are all smaller and in some ways less specialized than the rest of the New World monkeys. There is more about those in the next four pages.

FAMILY LIFE

Marmosets live in small family groups, often including a male and female with one or two growing young, sometimes in the company of two or three others, perhaps the young of previous years. Tamarins usually move in larger groups of up to 40 individuals.

Within their groups, both marmosets and tamarins constantly call to each other, forage together, and sit together on branches, squabbling mildly and grooming each other's fur in a companionable way. Young are born at any time of the year. Mothers usually give birth to twins, which both parents carry on their backs for several weeks, until they are strong enough to keep up with the group. The young reach independence at four to five months. Females are ready to mate again within three or four weeks of giving birth, so each pair may raise more than one litter per year.

Where do they live?

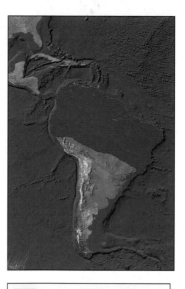

Marmosets and tamarins

Marmosets live in the dense rain forests of southern and eastern Brazil, mainly south of the Amazon River. The different species of tamarins are scattered widely across northern South America. Cottontops range as far north as Colombia and Panama, while golden lion tamarins are restricted to two or three small areas of mountain forest in eastern Brazil.

Neither marmosets nor tamarins are as plentiful as they once were. Huge areas of rain forests, drier mountain forests and grasslands that once spread almost continuously across South America have been cleared to provide farmland for expanding human populations and timber for export, destroying the homes and feeding territories of many kinds of wild animals, including primates. Several species are severely reduced, and likely to disappear as the clearance continues (see page 42-43).

Almost all-white lion tamarin

GROOMING

When monkeys of all kinds are at peace with the world and have nothing more urgent to do, they sit together and preen each other's fur. Using their fingers and teeth, they comb and pick out particles— dried skin, seeds, bits of twig, and such parasites as fleas and lice. This benefits both. The one preening seems to enjoy the activity, and the one who is preened ends up with cleaner fur and skin. However, it is also a form of bonding, in which two individuals come close and relax in each other's company, without wasting energy in distrust or aggression.

NEW WORLD AND OLD WORLD MONKEYS

New World and Old World monkeys differ physically in several small but important ways. The most obvious difference is in their faces. New World monkeys tend to have flat noses, with nostrils that open sideways. Those of the Old World have longer noses, sometimes with a central ridge, always with the nostrils opening forward like a dog's, or downwards like our own. New World monkeys have three molar or grinding teeth in both jaws on either side, while Old World monkeys (like apes and humans) have only two. Old World monkeys often have hard bony patches on their buttocks. New World monkeys never have.

Common marmoset

THE SMALLEST MONKEYS

Pygmy marmosets *(Cebuella pygmaea)* are similar to common marmosets and their kin, but much smaller. Smallest of all the monkeys, fully grown pygmy marmosets are only about 7 in (17 cm) long. They live in the forests of the northwestern Amazon basin, from northern Bolivia to eastern Ecuador.

NEW WORLD MONKEYS 2

Capuchins, douroucoulis and titi monkeys.

FACT FILE

BLACK-CAPPED CAPUCHIN

Suborder:	Anthropoidea
Family:	Cebidae
Scientific name:	*Cebus apella*
Color:	Dark brown-gray, with black cap, forearms, lower legs and tail
Weight:	Males 7.7 lb (3.5 kg), females 6.6 lb (3.0 kg)
Length, head and body:	Males 20 in (50 cm), females 18 in (45cm)
Habitat:	Tropical and mountain rain forest
Range:	Southern Brazil

DOUROUCOULI

Suborder:	Anthropoidea
Family:	Cebidae
Scientific name:	*Aotus trivirgatus*
Color:	Gray-brown back and flanks, golden yellow underparts; white face with dark muzzle
Weight:	2.2 lb (1 kg)
Length, head and body:	14 in (36 cm)
Habitat:	Tropical forests
Range:	Northwestern South America

WHITE-HANDED TITI

Suborder:	Anthropoidea
Family:	Cebidae
Scientific name:	*Callicebus torquatus*
Color:	Dark reddish brown, with pale white or orange throat, white or pale yellow hands
Weight:	2.2 lb (1 kg)
Length, head and body:	16 in (40 cm)
Habitat:	Tropical rain forest
Range:	Northwestern South America

RELATIONSHIPS

These are some members of the great family of cebid monkeys of South America. The following pages show more species from different branches of the family. There are four species of capuchin monkeys, all rather similar, and three species of titi monkeys, which are closely related to the capuchins. There is just one species of douroucouli—strange, lone monkeys with large eyes and mournful voices, that sleep by day and hunt at night.

CAPUCHIN MONKEYS gained their name from the pointed crest on the back of their head, which looks like a monk's cowl, or "capuche." The four species have different arrangements of tufted fur around the head, giving them different facial expressions. These are lively, active little animals—closer to everyone's idea of a monkey than marmosets and tamarins. Black-capped capuchins live in bands of a dozen or more at all levels of the rain forest. They feed mainly on nuts, fruit and leaves, but also hunt actively for insects, frogs, lizards and birds.

Douroucoulis are more solitary and solemn. Where most monkeys are active by day, these forage at night. Shine a flashlight in the trees after dark, and you may see huge, owl-like eyes blinking in a flat, gray and white face—hence the alternative name, "owl monkeys." Foraging for insects, spiders, birds and small mammals is a silent business. Between bouts of hunting, the males call with an extraordinary range of howls and hoots produced from a resonating chamber attached to the windpipe in their throat. The calls—from which they get their name—help to keep other douroucoulis at a distance, so they avoid hunting over the same ground.

Titi monkeys, like capuchins, are lively and active by day. While some inhabit tangled, lowland jungles and wet, even swampy, rain forest, the white-handed titis shown here seem to prefer drier, upland forests, at all levels from near ground to treetops. These are also called "widow monkeys," because widows in mourning in the countries where they live often wear white gloves and throat scarf or headdress. Titis feed mainly on nuts and fruit, but also hunt insects and small reptiles, birds and mammals. Intelligent and inquisitive, they use their hands with opposable thumbs (see page 19) to grasp and examine objects.

Capuchin monkey grasping a snake

FAMILY LIFE

Capuchin monkeys live in family groups of up to a dozen, sometimes joining to form bands of 40 or more. They live in large territories, which they patrol every day among the branches, with regular feeding and watering stations. They breed throughout the year, producing single young which both parents tend and carry.

Douroucoulis and titi monkeys are less sociable, living alone or in small family groups of three or four. Each group holds a feeding territory of a few square kilometers, from which it excludes neighbors as much as possible by calling, and occasionally by threatening or fighting. They, too, produce single young, which both parents care for, usually for about a year.

White-throated capuchin

PREDATORS

New World monkeys that live near the ground are in constant danger from snakes and several different kinds of wild forest cats. Those that forage higher in trees are sometimes taken by eagles and other large predatory birds. Another important predator is man. Some of these monkeys are good to eat. Living in groups provides protection—more pairs of eyes are watching, and more ears listening, for signs of danger.

Titi

Douroucouli

Where do they live?

Capuchins are widely distributed in rain forests on both sides of the Andes, from Panama in the north to northern Argentina, and they are also found in Trinidad. Black-capped capuchins live in the western Amazon basin, in both the hot, damp jungles bordering the rivers and in drier mountain forests up to about 10,000 ft (3,000 m) above sea level. Within this range live several subspecies, which have slightly different coloring and adaptations for living in different climates, with different foods available to them.

Douroucoulis, too, have a wide distribution, from northern Panama to Argentina and Paraguay. Titi monkeys live in the Amazon basin, particularly south of the great river and among its headwaters. White-handed titis occur mostly on mountain slopes along the eastern flank of the Andes.

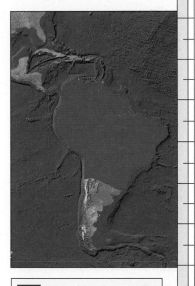

Capuchins, douroucoulis and titi monkeys

Dusky titi

Douroucouli

PREHENSILE TAILS

Most South American monkeys have long, muscular prehensile tails—tails with a tip that can curl around and grasp, like a finger. Some swing by their tails, but the kinds shown here use them mainly for grasping and balance. Capuchins can pick up nuts, peanut-sized or larger, in the tips of their tails, throw them in the air and catch them by hand. Titis crouch on a branch with all four feet close together, like a cat, and the tail hanging down behind. The heavy tail, almost as long as the body, acts as a counterweight, helping to hold the body upright, or the tip can wrap around a nearby branch for support.

When two titis—a mother and half-grown young, for example—sit close together, they may intertwine their tails like a rope. Each seems to feel safer in holding on that way.

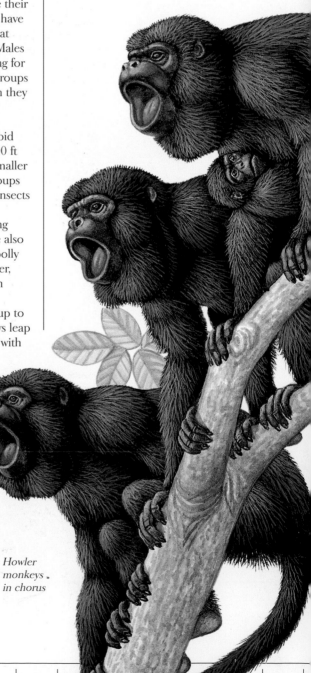

NEW WORLD MONKEYS 3

Squirrel, howler, saki, uakari, spider and woolly monkeys.

FACT FILE

BLACK HOWLER MONKEY

Suborder:	Anthropoidea
Family:	Cebidae
Scientific name:	*Alouatta caraya*
Color:	Females and young gray-brown, males entirely black
Weight:	14 lb (6.5 kg)
Length, head and body:	Males 8 in (20 cm)
Habitat:	Tropical rain forest
Range:	Central South America

COMMON SQUIRREL MONKEY

Suborder:	Anthropoidea
Family:	Cebidae
Scientific name:	*Saimiri sciureus*
Color:	Greenish-fawn back, paler below, white face with black muzzle
Weight:	Males 2.2 lb (1 kg), females 1.5 lb (700 g)
Length, head and body:	males 14 in (35 cm), females 11 in (28 cm)
Habitat:	Tropical rain forest
Range:	Panama and South America

BLACK-HANDED SPIDER MONKEY

Suborder:	Anthropoidea
Family:	Cebidae
Scientific name:	*Ateles geoffroyi*
Color:	Brown, with pale underparts, darker hands and feet
Weight:	16.5 lb (7.5 kg)
Length, head and body:	20 in (50 cm)
Habitat:	Tropical forest
Range:	Mexico to Panama

HOWLERS, AMONG THE LARGER AND HEAVIER of the South American monkeys, live in troops of up to 20. They prefer large trees with strong branches, and each troop needs plenty of room to feed. While several kinds of monkeys gibber and shriek to announce their presence and keep others away, howlers have specially developed bony voice boxes that enable them to howl or roar in chorus. Males are particularly noisy, their voices carrying for hundreds of meters through the trees. Groups roar especially around sunrise, and when they meet other troops. They feed mainly on young leaves and fruit.

Squirrel monkeys, smallest of the cebid monkeys, live in forests up to about 1,000 ft (300 m) above sea level, rarely higher. Smaller and quieter than howlers, they live in groups of 30–40, taking a variety of buds, fruit, insects and other small animals.

Spider monkeys are slender, with long arms and legs. Their fingers and toes are also extended, and they have no thumbs. Woolly monkeys are similar but fatter, with longer, denser fur. Biggest of all South American monkeys are woolly spider monkeys *(Brachyteles arachnoides)*, which weigh up to 26 lb (12 kg). Spider and woolly monkeys leap and swing through the trees, holding on with hands, feet and prehensile tail.

Saki and uakari monkeys, though closely related, are strikingly different in appearance. Both have long fur and bushy tails, but sakis have dense manes and facial hair, while uakaris are almost completely bald, with bare faces either black or brilliant red. They leap—almost fly—through the treetops, feeding mainly on fruit and nuts.

White-faced saki

Howler monkeys in chorus

FAMILY LIFE

These are all sociable species of monkeys, living in troops that travel and feed together in close company. Often a troop consists of a core of females with babies and young, with loosely attached attendant males. Mature males lead the troops through the forest, and make most noise when they encounter rival troops. The males are ready to mate with the females as they come on heat, but take no part in rearing the young. The gestation period (from mating to birth) is 7 to 8 months. Females bear single babies, carrying them for several weeks on their backs.

Common woolly monkey and young

RELATIONSHIPS

These are all monkeys that live in the tropical forests of Central or South America. Biologists cannot agree on how many species there are of each, or how to classify them. There are usually thought to be five or six species of howlers, and two of squirrel monkeys. Sakis and uakaris, probably closely related to each other, have three or four species each. Spider and woolly monkeys, too, are very close kin, with about seven species.

Spider monkey

Squirrel monkey

Where do they live?

Howler monkeys reach their northern limit in southern Mexico, and their southern limit in Argentina, Paraguay and eastern Brazil. Black howlers live in a central region of South America including parts of southern Brazil, Paraguay and Bolivia. Squirrel monkeys extend from this same southern region to the north coast of South America, and on into western Panama and Costa Rica. Spider monkeys, too, are widespread from southern Mexico to the Amazon basin. Woolly monkeys, uakaris and saki monkeys have more restricted ranges in different areas of the Amazon basin.

In many of these areas several species of monkeys overlap, sometimes competing for food, sometimes feeding side by side but on the different kinds of food that grow in the same area. So rich are these forests that there is usually plenty for all. Though monkeys tend to be hostile to other troops within their own species, they

▮ Squirrel, howler, saki, uakari, spider and woolly monkeys

often mix quite amicably with troops of different species. Each species quickly learns to respond to the alarm calls of the other. Even if they are competing for food, they benefit by the extra pairs of ears and eyes on the lookout for danger.

Red uakari

Spider monkey

OPPOSABLE THUMBS

When you hold a pencil, plate or screwdriver, your fingers and thumbs take opposite sides and grasp it between them. Can you do that with your toes? Some people can, but most cannot. Big toes are not opposable in the same way as thumbs. Few other animals have opposable thumbs. Though in nearly all primates the thumbs are separate from the fingers and almost as long, not all primates can use them in opposable fashion.

This is a simple but very important feature that allows some primates—including ourselves—to hold objects, turn them over, roll them around, examine them, take them to pieces, and perhaps think about how they work.

Some monkeys without opposable thumbs, such as howlers, sakis and uakaris, pick up small objects instead between their second and third fingers. Try it, and you will find that you can pick things up, but not examine them half as well as you can with an opposable thumb.

MACAQUES, BARBARY "APES" AND MANGABEYS

Old World monkeys of Asia, Gibraltar and Africa.

FACT FILE

JAPANESE MACAQUE

Suborder:	Anthropoidea
Family:	Cercopithecidae
Subfamily:	Cercopithecinae
Scientific name:	*Macaca fuscata*
Color:	Gray-brown fur, pink face
Weight:	18-40 lb (8-18 kg)
Length, head and body:	20 in (50 cm)
Habitat:	Forest and open ground
Range:	Japan

BARBARY "APE"

Suborder:	Anthropoidea
Family:	Cercopithecidae
Subfamily:	Cercopithecinae
Scientific name:	*Macaca sylvanus*
Color:	Reddish brown
Weight:	24-33 lb (11-15 kg)
Length, head and body:	20 in (50 cm)
Habitat:	Forest, scrub and grassland
Range:	Morocco, Algeria, Gibraltar

WHITE-COLLARED MANGABEY

Suborder:	Anthropoidea
Family:	Cercopithecidae
Subfamily:	Cercopithecinae
Scientific name:	*Cercocebus torquatus*
Color:	Gray, with white collar, dark face and white eyebrows
Weight:	22 lb (10 kg)
Length, head and body:	24 in (60 cm)
Habitat:	Tropical rain forest
Range:	Ghana, Nigeria, Cameroon and Gabon

MACAQUE IS THE GENERAL name for about 16 species of monkeys that live across northern Africa and Asia. They live in all kinds of environments, from tropical forests to cold mountain scrub, some almost entirely in trees, others mainly on the ground. The tree-living species tend to have long tails, the ground-living ones short tails or none at all. They eat whatever food is around, from fruit and shoots in the forest to farm produce and refuse in cities. When macaques—indeed all cercopithecines—find food, they stuff handfuls of it into their large cheek pouches, then race off to a quiet corner to sort it carefully at leisure.

Japanese macaques have thick gray-brown fur, which keeps them warm in bitterly cold winters. Their faces are bare, their tails only about one-quarter as long as the body. Formerly widespread in the temperate forests of Japan, they have declined with the spread of human populations and farming..

Barbary "apes" are not really apes. They have been misnamed; in fact they are tailless monkeys that live in scattered groups in the mountains of northwest Africa. A small population inhabits the fortress peninsula of Gibraltar, just across the Strait of Gibraltar (see opposite page).

Mangabeys are slender monkeys of African tropical forests, with tails longer than their head and body. Some are black or dark brown. Others, like the one illustrated, are splashed with patches of bright color. Their white eyebrows flash when they are frightened or threatening. They feed both in the trees and on the ground, mainly on nuts and fruit.

Barbary "apes," a species of macaque

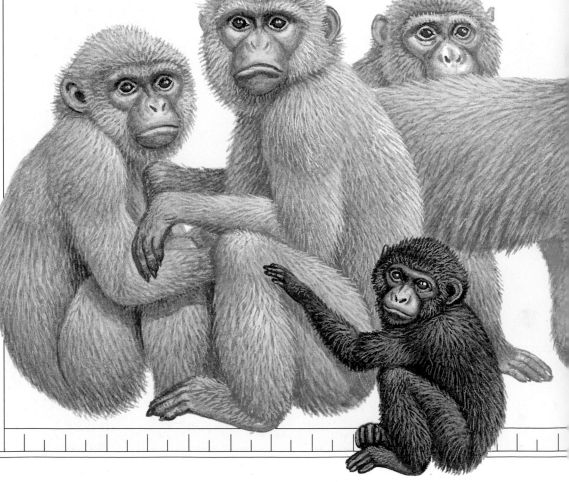

Rhesus macaques

RELATIONSHIPS

Old World monkeys are all included in the single family Cercopithecidae (Serco-pithy-*si*-dee), but fall into two subfamily groups. The subfamily Cercopithecinae (Serco-pithy-*si*-nee) includes the macaques, mangabeys, guenons, baboons, mandrills and their kin, which are illustrated here and on the next two double-page spreads. The subfamily Colobinae (Colo-*bi*-nee) includes the colobus and leaf monkeys and their kin, which are featured on pages 26–29.

Macaques include rhesus monkeys, Barbary "apes," which are not apes at all, and many other well-known species. The four kinds of mangabeys are African cousins, larger and heavier, but similar to macaques and closely related.

FAMILY LIFE

Macaques live in troops ranging in size from a few dozen to hundreds—in general, the better the feeding, the bigger the troop. In the tropics, where food is usually plentiful, they breed at any time of year. In Japan, China and other areas where winters can be intensely cold, they mate in autumn, producing their single babies during early summer.

Mangabeys also live in troops, but usually smaller ones, often of only one or up to three or four males and nine to a dozen females with young. They breed throughout the year, the females producing single babies, which cling to their fur and ride on their backs. Group living helps to protect them from ground predators, especially lions, leopards and other cats that try to creep up unseen.

Agile mangabey

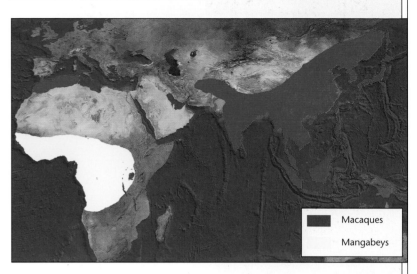

Where do they live?

Macaques

Mangabeys

Macaques have the widest distribution of any group of monkeys, though the different species occupy narrower areas within this span. They are found from Morocco to the East Indies, as far north as Tibet and Japan. Small to medium-sized monkeys, they have many local names. From northern India to China they are rhesus monkeys, in southern India bonnet macaques, in Sri Lanka toque monkeys, in the East Indies crab-eating monkeys and in northern Africa and Gibraltar Barbary "apes." Japanese macaques have a relatively limited distribution in Japan itself. Mangabeys live in the tropical forests of west and central Africa. White-collared mangabeys are found in a limited area of southern Nigeria, Cameroon and Gabon.

MONKEYS FOR MEDICAL RESEARCH

Rhesus monkeys, small and relatively easy to keep in captivity, have for many years been exported from India to medical laboratories all over the world. Though laboratories have bred them too, it has generally been easier and cheaper to buy them from suppliers, who in turn buy them from hunters and trappers. Similar to humans in some of their physiology and body chemistry, rhesus monkeys have contributed to many important medical discoveries, including blood-typing and the development of vaccines.

People concerned with animal welfare want to stop the trade, claiming that it is cruel and that thousands of monkeys die each year before they ever reach the laboratories. Researchers point to the progress made, and the number of human lives saved, by having rhesus and other monkeys available for research.

Should monkeys be caught, traded and used in this way? What do you think?

MACAQUES OF GIBRALTAR

The Barbary macaques on the British colony of Gibraltar are the only wild monkeys in Europe. Their ancestors may have included the last remnants of a much larger European population, but numbers today are

boosted from time to time by imports from Africa. According to a centuries-old tradition, if the "apes" leave the Rock of Gibraltar, Britain will lose its colony. So the British government looks after them. Though wild, they are in the care of the British garrison, and are a pampered tourist attraction.

Japanese macaque—these hardy monkeys are good swimmers and bathe in hot springs when it snows

AFRICAN GROUND-LIVING MONKEYS

Baboons, mandrills, drills and geladas.

FACT FILE

HAMADRYAS BABOON

Suborder:	Anthropoidea
Family:	Cercopithecidae
Subfamily:	Cercopithecinae
Scientific name:	*Papio hamadryas*
Color:	Brown, males with gray cape, red face and buttocks
Weight:	Males 33 lb (15 kg), females 22 lb (10 kg)
Length, head and body:	30 in (75 cm)
Habitat:	Desert scrub, grassland
Range:	Northeastern Africa, Arabia

MANDRILL

Suborder:	Anthropoidea
Family:	Cercopithecidae
Subfamily:	Cercopithecinae
Scientific name:	*Mandrillus sphinx*
Color:	Gray-brown back, paler underparts, blue cheeks, red nose, blue buttocks
Weight:	Males 55 lb (25 kg), females 26 lb (12 kg)
Length, head and body:	28–31 in (70–80 cm)
Habitat:	Rain forest edge
Range:	Cameroon, Congo, DR Congo, Gabon

DRILL

Suborder:	Anthropoidea
Family:	Cercopithecidae
Subfamily:	Cercopithecinae
Scientific name:	*Mandrillus leucophaeus*
Color:	Dark brown body, black face, white beard, blue buttocks
Weight:	Males 100 lb (45 kg), females smaller
Length, head and body:	28 in (70 cm)
Habitat:	Rain forest edge
Range:	Nigeria, Cameroon

GELADA

Suborder:	Anthropoidea
Family:	Cercopithecidae
Subfamily:	Cercopithecinae
Scientific name:	*Theropithecus gelada*
Color:	Dark to paler brown body, cape over shoulders, red skin on neck and buttocks
Weight:	Males 44 lb (20 kg), females 31 lb (14 kg)
Length, head and body:	28 in (70 cm)
Habitat:	Open grassland, scrub
Range:	Ethiopia

THESE ARE ALL AFRICAN ground-living monkeys. Some live in forests, others in open woodland or scrub, others again in grassland and semidesert where there is not a tree for miles. Females and young spend more time in the trees, while heavier males use their weight to push through dense undergrowth. When danger threatens, they all climb nimbly, shinning up trees or cliffs faster than snakes or cats can follow, and barking loudly from the top to warn the world of predators. They roost in high places at night. During the day you are just as likely to see them on the ground, scrabbling and searching for their favorite foods—seeds, nuts, grass, new shoots, fresh leaves, insect, birds and small mammals.

Though the name "hamadryas" comes from a word meaning "tree-spirit," Hamadryas baboons live in semidesert areas of Egypt and Arabia, mainly in dry, open woodland and grassy plains. Early Egyptians regarded them as wise and sacred, training them to live in their houses and temples, and preserving them as mummies after death. Other species of baboons live in similar dry habitats, extending over much of southern and western Africa.

Mandrills and drills are heavyweight baboons of tropical forests. They live mainly on the ground, but take to the sturdy lower branches of the trees for traveling and safety. Both have drab, gray-brown body fur. In drills this extends to the face, enlivened by a smart white beard and collar. Mandrills by contrast

Hamadryas baboon

Gelada

are brightly decorated, with golden beard and collar, blue grooved cheeks and vivid red nose. Both species have bright sky-blue buttocks—in male mandrills the colour extends to the genitalia.

Geladas, too, are heavyweights. They live on treeless plateaus of Ethiopia. Though their fur is drab, they have patches of pink wattled skin on the chest and buttocks, which brighten in females that are ready to mate. At rest, the face is dark, but a male threatening his neighbors exposes vivid white eyebrows and peels back his upper lip, showing pink gums and a formidable set of teeth. Geladas feed mainly on grass, which they pluck by hand, and on fruit, roots, flowers and leaves.

Drill

FAMILY LIFE

Baboons, mandrills, drills and geladas live in troops of up to about 20, dominated by a single old male but including several females, young and immature males, which patrol widely over extensive feeding

Baby baboon eating fruit

areas. At times these band together into much larger groups, perhaps to share a sudden superabundance of fruit or grass. Troops often congregate at night among trees and on cliffs where they can sleep safely.

These species all breed throughout the year, with no marked seasons. Females have menstrual cycles of four to five weeks, often indicating the midpoint of the cycle—the few days when they are most fertile—by a change in color of the buttocks. Gestation takes between 24 and 28 weeks, producing single babies, rarely twins.

Mandrill

Where do they live?

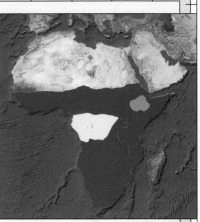

Baboons are widespread throughout Africa south of the Sahara desert, extending into the western tip of Arabia. Hamadryas baboons occupy only the dry northeastern corner of this range, including parts of Egypt, Sudan, Ethiopia, Somalia and Yemen.

Mandrills live in the forests of Cameroon, mainland Equatorial Guinea, Gabon and Congo, and drills are found in northern Cameroon, Nigeria, and on Bioko, a forested island in the Gulf of Guinea. Geladas live only on high grasslands in the northern and central mountains of Ethiopia.

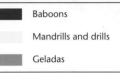

■	Baboons
▫	Mandrills and drills
■	Geladas

Male mandrill snarling

RELATIONSHIPS

Here is a group of monkeys, closely related and similar in appearance, that spend much of their time on the ground. Strongly built, short-tailed or tailless, they stare at the world and each other down long, doglike muzzles, from deep-set eyes under heavy brow ridges. Males of each species are noticeably larger than females, with longer and more dangerous-looking canine teeth. There are five species of baboons, one each of mandrills, drills and geladas.

GROUND LIVING

Dominant baboon trying to stand upright

We know baboons and their kin are not immediate ancestors of man. But they have taken the first important step that more direct ancestors must have taken— coming down from the trees, and starting to find ways of living on open ground, away from the forest edge.

They walk or scramble on all fours, using their fingers as toes, and cannot stand upright as we can. But when feeding they sit back on their haunches, freeing their hands for plucking, grasping, digging, and examining what they have found. This is a second important step, leading to a clearer understanding of the world around them.

SOME AFRICAN FOREST MONKEYS

Guenons, talapoins and patas monkeys.

FACT FILE

MUSTACHED GUENON

Suborder:	Anthropoidea
Family:	Cercopithecidae
Subfamily:	Cercopithecinae
Scientific name:	*Cercopithecus cephus*
Color:	Brown back, blue-gray or white underparts, face blue with yellow cheeks and ears, white 'mustache'
Weight:	4.4 lb (2 kg)
Length, head and body:	20 in (50 cm)
Habitat:	Tropical forest
Range:	Cameroon, Gabon, Central African Republic

DIANA MONKEY

Suborder:	Anthropoidea
Family:	Cercopithecidae
Subfamily:	Cercopithecinae
Scientific name:	*Cercopithecus diana*
Color:	Back black or blue-gray, face varied, beard, chest and throat white, reddish flanks with white stripe on thigh
Weight:	4.4 lb (2 kg)
Length, head and body:	20 in (50 cm)
Habitat:	Tropical forest
Range:	Sierra Leone to Ghana

TALAPOIN MONKEY

Suborder:	Anthropoidea
Family:	Cercopithecidae
Subfamily:	Cercopithecinae
Scientific name:	*Miopithecus talapoin*
Color:	Gray-green or yellow back, paler underparts, gray face with brown cheeks
Weight:	3 lb (1.4 kg)
Length, head and body:	14 in (36 cm)
Habitat:	Lowland and swamp forests
Range:	Cameroon to Angola, western Africa

MEDIUM-SIZED MONKEYS, with long limbs and a tail longer than the head and body, guenons live in troops of a dozen or more that move through the forest in a constant, chattering search for food and excitement. They are the most colorful of all monkeys, basically brown or gray, but decorated with red, white or golden fur, and flashes of red, white or blue skin. These decorations are found particularly on the head, face and neck, and on the rump, buttocks and genital regions—the areas that show when they are active in the trees. Males are usually larger than females.

Mustached guenons, shown here, have a striking color scheme of black-tinged brown fur, with reddish brown on the rump and tail, white underparts and multi-colored face. Other guenons include species with white noses and ear tufts, golden cheeks, blue faces, red noses and ears, and many more variations. By these features, members of the different species can quickly recognize each other on sight.

Talapoin monkeys, a size smaller than guenons, live in low swampy forest, never far from water. They often feed and roost in the low canopy overhanging rivers and lakes. While all monkeys can swim when they need to, talapoins seem to regard swimming as part of their way of life, leaping into the water to avoid predators, to catch food, or possibly just to cool down.

Patas monkeys (for Fact File, see page 12) by contrast prefer dry forest, savannah, scrub, and even dry, sandy desert. Long-tailed and long-limbed like guenons, they live mainly on the ground, climbing trees or cliffs only for safety or to see farther. Unlike guenons they stand and walk upright on their hind legs, using the tail as a prop. If chased by a predator, they get down on all fours and run. They have been clocked at (30 mph) 50 km per hour and more. Patas monkeys can outrun most small cats. By twisting, turning, and eventually climbing to safety, they can even outsmart lions, leopards and cheetahs.

Talapoin

Mustached guenon

Where do they live?

Patas monkeys drinking at a pool

RELATIONSHIPS

Guenon is a general name for about 20 species of monkeys grouped in the genus *Cercopithecus*—the ones for which the family and subfamily are named. These are Africa's commonest monkeys, the different species occurring in a wide variety of forests from dripping jungle to dry woodlands and savannah. Talapoins are similar to guenons, but smaller, with a marked preference for swamp forest. Patas monkeys round off the group, clearly related to guenons, but ground-living and remarkably fast when they run on all fours.

Guenons occupy a wide swath of central and southern Africa. Most widespread is the green or vervet monkey, *Cercopithecus aethiops*, which is found from the southern edge of the Sahara desert to the Sudan and Ethiopia, and south to Cape Province. Moustached guenons have a comparatively limited range in the forests of Gabon, Cameroon, Central African Republic and Congo, north of the Congo (Zaire) River. Other species are scattered across central Africa from the west coast to the Rift Valley.

The two species of talapoins divide the lowland forests of western central Africa between them, from Cameroon in the north to Angola in the south. Patas monkeys live in the dry savannah zone—between deserts to the north and forests to the south—that runs across northern Africa from Senegal to Sudan, ranging south into Uganda, Kenya and Tanzania.

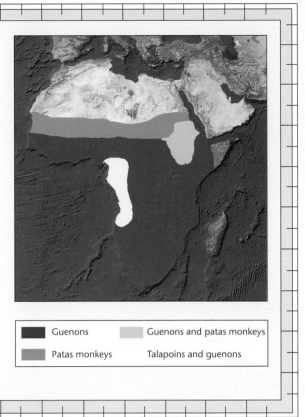

■ Guenons	Guenons and patas monkeys
Patas monkeys	Talapoins and guenons

FAMILY LIFE

Guenons live in troops of between 12 and 20, each centered in a home range but feeding in larger territories where several groups may overlap. Troops include two or three adult males, four or five adult females, mostly with babies, and as many immature young. Members of the troop roost together at night and forage together

Talapoin mother with young

by day, maintaining a constant watch for predators. On the ground their main enemies are snakes and cats. In the treetops they fall prey to eagles.

Guenons breed at any time of

the year. For the first few weeks of life, the single baby clings to its mother's fur, then later rides piggyback until it can keep up with the troop.

Talapoins have a similar social life, though their troops usually number 50–100 or more. Females give birth to unusually large offspring, weighing one-fifth as much as the mother.

Patas monkeys run in troops of up to 12, each dominated by a single adult male. Males in this species are notably bigger than females. Troop leaders use their bulk to threaten and keep away rival males.

Diana monkey

DIVIDING THE FOREST

Tropical forests tend to be tall, with distinct layers. The tallest trees form a high canopy around 150 ft (45 m). Lesser trees form a lower canopy around 100 ft (30 m), and others fill up the space below, down to a layer of shrubs and a tangle of undergrowth. The Diana monkey (pictured left) feeds high in the tallest trees, the mustached guenon at much lower levels, and other species in the middle layers. However, nearly all climb to bed at night, seeking the comparative safety of the higher branches.

Patas monkey testing a possible bed

COLOBUS MONKEYS OF AFRICA

Leaf-eating monkeys of African forests.

FACT FILE

SATANIC BLACK COLOBUS MONKEY

Suborder:	Anthropoidea
Family:	Cercopithecidae
Subfamily:	Colobinae
Scientific name:	*Colobus satanas*
Color:	Back, head and face entirely black
Weight:	22 lb (10 kg)
Length, head and body:	28 in (70 cm)
Habitat:	Tropical forest
Range:	Cameroon, Equatorial Guinea, Gabon and Congo

GUINEA RED COLOBUS MONKEY

Suborder:	Anthropoidea
Family:	Cercopithecidae
Subfamily:	Colobinae
Scientific name:	*Colobus badius*
Color:	Reddish brown back and head, pale cream underparts
Weight:	18 lb (8 kg)
Length, head and body:	24 in (60 cm)
Habitat:	Tropical forest
Range:	Senegal, Gambia and Ghana

RELATIONSHIPS

These are medium-sized African forest monkeys, reddish brown or black, with big stomachs and spindly limbs and tails. The name "colobus," meaning mutilated or deformed, refers to their hands, in which the thumbs are very small or absent. Biologists cannot agree on classification within the group. Some say there are two species, each with many subspecies. Others say the variations are enough to justify six or seven separate species, some with subspecies as well. This book follows the classification that assigns six species within the genus *Colobus*, and a seventh, the olive colobus monkey, in a separate genus of its own.

COLOBUS MONKEYS are slightly bigger than guenons, but quieter, more placid, and less likely to create disturbance. In a treeful of monkeys, where groups of both are present, you are likely to notice the guenons immediately, from their lively movements and chattering. Only gradually will you see or hear colobus monkeys among them. Colobus monkeys lack the brilliant colors of guenons. Some are all black or starkly black and white, others are reddish brown, while olive colobus are a handsome but unexciting khaki green.

A more fundamental difference, though less obvious, is a different approach to feeding. This is based on the fact that colobus monkeys eat leaves, rather than buds, shoots and fruit, so sit quietly and browse in the densest vegetation they can find.

The satanic black colobus shown here is one of four predominantly black monkeys. All of these have black faces ringed with white, and—except for one form—patches of long white fur on their shoulders or flanks. In some, the tails thicken to a distinct white tuft at the end. Since they were first hunted, the all-black or black-and-white furs of colobus monkeys have been valued for decoration. From medieval times onward many hundreds of thousands were exported from central and western Africa, commanding good prices in world markets.

Red colobus monkeys are one of two species with reddish brown fur. The other species, Kirk's colobus, has white instead of cream underparts, a pale nose, and dark brown or black feet. Fortunately for them, red skins were valued far less than black, so red colobus monkeys were spared intensive hunting.

All the colobus monkeys spend most of their time in forest trees, browsing on leaves, fruit and other vegetation, seldom bothering to descend to ground level.

Guinea red colobus monkeys

Satanic black colobus monkey of west Africa

Where do they live?

Black-and-white colobus

DIGESTING TOUGH LEAVES

Unlike cercopithecine monkeys (see, for example, macaques on pages 20–21), colobus monkeys have no cheek pouches for storing their food. They are equipped instead to eat tough leaves, grass and shoots, as well as softer ones, that other monkeys cannot digest. So they have more complex molar (back) teeth to grind up the food, big salivary glands producing plenty of liquid to wash it down, and a stomach with separate chambers, like that of a cow or sheep, in which bacteria break down and digest the plant material. Macaques and guenons stuff their cheeks with food and are ready to run with it. Colobus monkeys, like cows, browse quietly and take their time over feeding. Like cows, too, they generate gases in their stomach, getting rid of them by frequent belching.

FAMILY LIFE

Both the black and the red varieties of colobus monkeys live in troops, usually consisting of one or two mature males and several females. Black colobus troops of this size defend feeding territories. The males roar at dawn, dusk and at intervals through the day to demonstrate possession, but seldom find the need to defend themselves against intruders. Olive colobus troops are of similar size. Troops of red colobus monkeys tend to be larger, probably by loose amalgamation of several small

Colobus quietly browsing up a tree

troops. Large or small, colobus groups seem to live peaceably among themselves and with neighbors.

Colobus monkeys breed throughout the year, producing single young. Black colobus babies at birth are covered with gray or white woolly fur, to which females other than their mothers respond maternally while they are small. They gain their black and white fur at three to four months. Red and olive colobus babies are paler than their parents, but similar in pattern, and are guarded almost exclusively by their mothers. Uniquely among primates, olive colobus mothers carry their babies in their mouths for the first few days after birth.

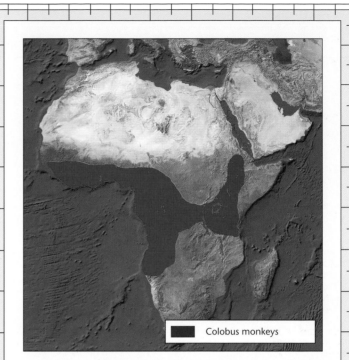

Colobus monkeys

Colobus monkeys extend in a broad belt from Guinea, on the west coast of Africa, south to Angola and northern Namibia, and east to DR Congo, Uganda, Tanzania, Kenya and Ethiopia. Black colobus monkeys live in the rainforests of Cameroon, Rio Equatorial Guinea, Gabon and Congo. Red colobus live in Senegal, Gambia and Ghana. Olive colobus are found only in Sierra Leone, Guinea, Togo and Nigeria.

NO THUMBS

On page 19 we saw the value of strong opposable thumbs, which allow some monkeys and apes, and ourselves, to grasp, turn and examine objects in our hands. Why have colobus monkeys very small thumbs, or none at all? Monkeys and apes that spend much of their lives brachiating (swinging from branches) usually have long fingers and long, narrow hands. In swinging, they keep the fingers together, using them as hooks. Try making your hand into a hook of this kind: what do you do with your thumb? It just gets in the way. So brachiators are probably better off with only small thumbs.

How did they come to lose them? Their ancestors may have had larger thumbs, but individuals with smaller ones fared better through the ages, and now they all have reduced thumbs.

Despite its small thumb, this colobus monkey has no trouble feeding itself

(see pages 18–19)

FACT FILE

BLACK GIBBON

Suborder:	Anthropoidea
Family:	Hylobatidae
Scientific name:	*Hylobates concolor*
Color:	Males, black head, body and face; females, pale head and body, black face
Weight:	11 lb (5 kg)
Length, head and body:	24 in (60 cm)
Habitat:	Tropical forest
Range:	Southern China, Laos, Cambodia, Vietnam

LAR (WHITE-HANDED) GIBBON

Suborder:	Anthropoidea
Family:	Hylobatidae
Scientific name:	*Hylobates lar*
Color:	Black, brown or tawny, with white hands
Weight:	11 lb (5 kg)
Length, head and body:	24 in (60 cm)
Habitat:	Tropical forest
Range:	Burma, south to Sumatra and Java

SIAMANG

Suborder:	Anthropoidea
Family:	Hylobatidae
Scientific name:	*Hylobates syndactylus*
Color:	Black with gray muzzle and beard
Weight:	22 lb (10 kg)
Length, head and body:	33 in (85 cm)
Habitat:	Tropical forest
Range:	Malay Peninsula, Sumatra

Siamang calling

APES: GIBBONS AND SIAMANGS

Swinging apes of the Asian forests.

ONE GROUP OF ASIAN APES, long-armed, broad-chested, and able to stand and walk upright, has specialized in tree-living. The gibbons and siamangs are slender, graceful acrobats which, in their ability to swing through the treetops, are a match for the howler and spider monkeys of South America (see pages 18–19). Formerly widespread in the forests of China and beyond, these small apes are currently restricted to islands and peninsulas of southeastern Asia. With six species, they are the most varied and versatile group of all the apes.

Unusually among monkeys and apes, male black gibbons are bright, glossy black, but females are pale, golden or gray brown, and babies are white for the first few weeks of their lives. Lar gibbons vary in color according to where they live. Siamangs, which are larger, heavier gibbons, are mostly black.

Gibbons feed mainly on ripe fruit. Young leaves are their second choice, and they also eat insects and other invertebrates.

You usually hear gibbons long before you see them, calling to each other with curiously melodious songs. The different species have different songs. If you can recognize a tune, you can tell the gibbons apart without seeing them.

Male and female black gibbons

Pileated gibbon

Siamang

Lar gibbon

RELATIONSHIPS

Are the animals on these pages monkeys? No. Although they climb and swing among the branches like monkeys, they have no tails. That means that they can only be gibbons or siamangs, the apes that most resemble monkeys in general appearance and ways of life (see below right, "What's in a tail?").

Biologists see apes as monkeylike animals that spend much of their time on the ground. They have no need for a balancing tail. With their long forelimbs they can walk on all fours, with their weight resting on their knuckles. However, they can also stand upright and walk on their hind legs, leaving their forelimbs free to rotate and spread sideways. Their chests are broad and barrel-like, wrists and hands flexible, brains larger and more complex than in monkeys. Animals with these characteristics have existed for some 35–40 million years.

There are 10 different kinds of apes in the world. Here we separate the six species of gibbons and siamangs into one family, the Hylobatidae, keeping them apart from the "great apes"—the orangutans, gorillas and two kinds of chimpanzees that make up the family Pongidae.

Where do they live?

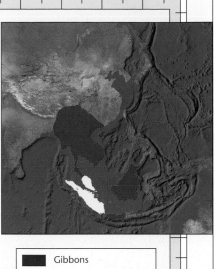

Gibbons as a group live in tall tropical forests from Assam (northeast India) and Burma in the north, through Yunnan (southern China), Thailand, Cambodia, Laos and Vietnam to Malaysia, and on through Sumatra, Java and Borneo. Throughout this wide range their forests are being felled for timber. Every year their world becomes smaller and more patchy.

Black gibbons are restricted mainly to China, Laos, eastern Cambodia and Vietnam—all areas of expanding human populations. Lar, or white-handed, gibbons have a wider distribution from mainland Burma, Thailand and the Malay Peninsula to the islands of Sumatra and Java. Siamangs are at home only in the Malay Peninsula and Sumatra.

■	Gibbons
■	Siamangs and gibbons

FAMILY LIFE

Gibbons live in small family groups, usually one adult pair with two or three juveniles. Pairs mate throughout the year, and single young are born after a gestation of about 30 weeks. Babies are fed on milk for over a year, then remain with their parents for five or six years. Both parents take an interest, male siamangs being especially attentive towards the youngsters, and keeping the family together.

Juvenile lar gibbon

WHAT'S IN A TAIL?

We have seen that most monkeys have tails, and that:
- Some have tails longer than their bodies (which ones?)
- Some have prehensile tails (which ones?)
- Some have short tails (which ones?)
- Some have lost their tails altogether (which ones?)

For monkeys that live in trees, tails are important to maintain balance, and in some cases to provide an extra grip. For those living on the ground, they are no longer needed. Apes probably began as monkeys that spent more and more time on the ground, and, in the course of time, lost their tails. Biologists think of gibbons and siamangs as apes that, having spent millions of years living on the ground, then returned to living in trees. Their arms and legs lengthened, they became as skilful as monkeys at swinging from bough to bough—but they never got their tails back.

THE GREAT APES OF AFRICA AND ASIA

Similarities and differences.

RELATIONSHIPS

There is only one living species of orangutan, with two populations that live in two separate localities of southeastern Asia. These differ from each other enough for biologists to call them separate subspecies. Similarly, there is only one species of gorilla, again with distinct populations, in this case three, forming separate subspecies. The two kinds of chimpanzees are at first sight very similar—about as similar as are the subspecies of gorilla. But they live in different areas and do not seem to interbreed. Biologists who have studied them both have no doubt that they form two distinct species.

Pygmy chimpanzee

FEEDING

Anthropoid, or great, apes all feed mainly on shoots and leaves. Orangutans and gorillas eat very little else. Because much of this material has very little nutritional value, they have to eat a lot of it, and spend nearly all of their time munching. In middle age they develop huge stomachs and massive intestines to hold and digest these bulky meals. In zoos, where there is usually plenty of food close at hand, they grow fatter, lazier and heavier than in the wild.

Chimpanzees feed mainly on vegetation, too, but they also eat insects and other kinds of animal foods, for which they have to hunt. More active than orangs and gorillas, both in the wild and in zoos, they stay slimmer well into middle age.

Orangutans, chimpanzees and gorillas are all larger and more heavily built than monkeys or gibbons. Big orangs and chimpanzees can stretch up as tall as small humans, and grow much heavier. Gorillas grow as tall as fully grown humans, and again weigh much more.

People tend to confuse the three species, perhaps because, more than any other animals, they look like humans, and we think of them all as distant—very distant—cousins. In fact they differ from each other in several easily spotted ways. For a start, orangutans are almost always reddish brown, but chimpanzees and gorillas are black or gray. Then, gorillas are much bigger than the others. And while you may see any of them both on the ground and in trees, orangs are mainly tree-living, and much more at home in the branches than either of the others. They also live only in southeastern Asia, while chimpanzees and gorillas live only in Africa.

Chimpanzees and gorillas look quite similar when they are very young, but both grow quickly, and gorillas soon begin to put on the solid bones and flesh of their species.

Of the three kinds of apes, chimpanzees seem to be the most intelligent—that is, mentally closest to humans and quickest in their ways of thinking, solving puzzles and making and using tools.

Gorilla (male)

Chimpanzee (male)

Early apes

An 11-year-old orangutan

This probably reflects their modes of living. Browsing on leaves makes few demands on the intellects of orangutans and gorillas. Chimpanzees spend part of their time hunting, which is far more demanding, and more likely to sharpen their wits.

FOSSIL MONKEYS AND APES

Fossils of monkeys, apes and early humans are never found complete. When the original animals died, other animals probably ate them, and their bones scattered, leaving only fragments of bones, incomplete skulls and bits of skeletons. Paleontologists who study these remnants may find only half a lower jaw with three or four teeth, the front or base of a skull, a fragment of pelvis or other piece of skeleton. There are usually several, scattered over a wide area, that may be from one animal or several animals. From these, using their knowledge of modern and fossil skeletons, the scientists have to "reconstruct," or build up, models of what the original animals looked like, and decide whether they were monkeys, apes or early humans. Sometimes this becomes guesswork, or at least a matter for different scientists to disagree over.

Orangutan (male)

During the past few million years there have been dozens of species of apelike animals. If they were alive today, we would call them great apes. Today we have only two species of chimpanzee and one species each of gorilla and orangutan. What happened to all the others? We do not know. Most of them are represented only in small fragments of jaws, teeth and other bones, seldom as complete skeletons. Some kinds were widespread and survived over millions of years. Others were more local, and seem to have died out more quickly.

Proconsul. The earliest fossil apes, found in east Africa and up to 20 million years old, include species grouped as *Proconsul*. Some were up to chimpanzee size, with large, projecting front teeth, large canines and small grinding teeth. They probably walked on all fours and spent at least part of their time in trees.

Australopithecus. Around 3 to 5 million years ago appeared several forms grouped under this name. They stood up to 5 ft (1.5 m) tall, with large front teeth and molars. They probably walked on two legs and spent most of their time on the ground. Some may have made and used primitive tools.

Paranthropus. From 1 to 2.5 million years ago lived several apes with broader faces, heavier jaws and more massive grinding teeth. Scientists group these as *Paranthropus.* They stood up to about 4 ft (1.2 m) tall and probably resembled small gorillas in appearance and way of life.

Chimpanzees. Very few fossils of chimpanzees (or of gorillas or orangutans) have been found, so we do not know how long they have existed.

Skull of Proconsul africanus

Skull of Australopithecus africanus

Skull of Paranthropus robustus

Skull of chimpanzee

GIGANTOPITHECUS

This was a group of large apes that lived up to about 1 million years ago. We know them only from fragments of jaws and teeth, which show that they were mainly vegetarian. However, they must have been enormous—much bigger than humans, and probably bigger than even the largest living gorillas. They probably died out long before the first humans appeared.

GREAT APES: ORANGUTANS

Lone "old man" of the Indonesian rainforests.

FACT FILE

Suborder:	Anthropoidea
Family:	Pongidae
Scientific name:	*Pongo pygmaeus*
Color:	Reddish brown to black
Weight:	Males 150 lb (70 kg), females 80 lb (35 kg)
Length, head and body:	Males 40 in (1 m), females 30 in (80 cm)
Habitat:	Trees and shrubs in rain forest
Range:	Borneo and Sumatra

Adult female orangutan

RELATIONSHIPS

Orangutans are large, often tubby and ponderous great apes of southeastern Asia. They are larger and heavier than monkeys, more spiderlike than chimpanzees, and far less bulky than gorillas. Like their gibbon cousins and neighbors, they are tree-living apes, though they lack gibbons' grace and agility. Where gibbons seem almost to fly through the treetops, orangutans swing like awkward, long-armed sacks among the lower branches, pausing to hang thoughtfully from one hand, and scratching with the other. The two localities in which they live, separated by wide and deep water, have given rise to two subspecies:

- Bornean orangutan, *Pongo pygmaeus pygmaeus*
- Sumatran orangutan, *Pongo pygmaeus abelii*

THE DENSE GREEN FORESTS of Indonesia are the home of several kinds of monkey and gibbons, and one kind of great ape—the orangutan. The name means "old man of the forest"—mature adults of either sex have the worn, stooped appearance of a small old man, with long, untidy hair, wrinkled skin and thin straggling beard.

On the ground, orangs walk clumsily on all fours, taking part of the weight on their short legs, and part on the longer arms. However, they spend as much time as possible in the trees, where they probably feel safer and more at home. Young ones climb and swing with skill and daring, grasping the branches with slender hands and fingerlike toes. Older ones, more heavy and solidly built, move slowly and deliberately, swinging with great care as though afraid of falling.

Orangutans feed mainly on fruit, including figs, mangoes, durians and plantains, of which different kinds ripen at different times of the year. If fruit is scarce, they eat insects, leaves, shoots and roots. Where local people grow crops and vegetables, orangutans sometimes make themselves unpopular by stealing, though normally they stay well away from farms and plantations. Occasionally they catch and eat lizards or birds.

Sumatran subspecies

Bornean subspecies

Where do they live?

Young captive orang

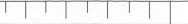

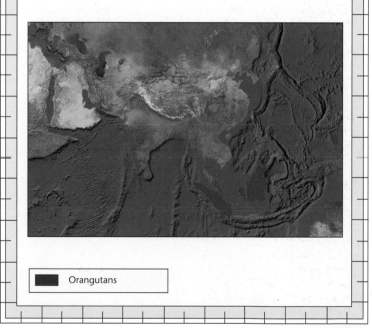

Adult male orang

FAMILY LIFE

Male orangutans are solitary animals who seem to prefer their own company to any other. Their loud roaring calls, amplified in large, pendulous throat pouches, echo through the forests, announcing their presence in a feeding range or territory they consider their own, and warning others to keep away. Ranges often overlap, so several males may find themselves feeding

Mother and baby orang

together when a particular tree bears its fruit. They seldom quarrel. If there is plenty for all, eating is more profitable than fighting. However, noisy quarrels and fights break out from time to time, and most old males bear bites, deep scratches and other battle scars.

Females, too, keep their own company, but usually have a baby or one or two juveniles up to six or seven years old in attendance. When ready for mating, a female responds positively to the call of a male, approaching and feeding with him in company. After mating several times, she wanders away, still leading her young from previous matings. Gestation takes about 38 weeks. The babies grow slowly, taking seven or more years to reach complete independence.

Orangutans once lived as far north as northern China, and as far west as India. As humans spread, orangs became easy prey. Many were hunted for food, and more disappeared as the forests were cleared for agriculture. Today we find them only on the islands of Sumatra and Borneo, living in the densest parts of the rain forest. Even there they are very much at risk, for their forests are being felled for timber, and without the forest, orangs cannot survive.

For the past 40 years Indonesia and other heavily forested countries have tried to improve the wealth and living conditions of their people by exploiting these forests, cutting down the trees and exporting the timber. In some parts of Indonesia this has resulted in severe losses of the primary (original) forest, which took many years to mature and will take many more years to recover. When the forest is cut, orangutans and monkeys lose their feeding territories. To find new ones they have to invade the territories of others, then perhaps move again a few weeks later as the cutting continues.

■ Orangutans

SCHOOL FOR ORANGUTANS

Baby orangutans are popular as pets in many parts of Indonesia. Though buying and selling them is illegal, hunters have for many years hunted mothers with babies, shooting the mothers and selling the babies into captivity. While still young, the orphans make friendly, responsive pets. As they grow older and stronger, they become bored, cross and destructive, more so if they are chained or confined to cages. Then their owners want to be rid of them. They cannot be released into the wild, because they have never learned how to forage for food, avoid predators or respond to other orangs.

Conservation groups in Borneo and Sumatra have been organized to rescue young orangs from captivity, bring them together in "schools" in the forest, and gradually get them used to foraging for themselves. After a few days in cages, they are released to wander, but lured back to the safety of the "school" by an evening feed. After a few weeks of learning, some set off on their own into the wild, others are taken to remote parts of the forest and released. Schooling does not guarantee their survival, but increases their chances of making a normal life for themselves.

GREAT APES: CHIMPANZEES

Our favorite apes, and nearest kin among the apes, chimpanzees live in central and west Africa.

FACT FILE

Suborder:	Anthropoidea
Family:	Pongidae
Scientific name:	*Pan troglodytes*
Color:	Thin dark brown to black fur, gray or pink skin
Weight:	90 lb (40 kg)
Length, head and body:	33 in (84 cm)
Habitat:	Tropical rain forest and grassland
Range:	West, central and eastern Africa

RELATIONSHIPS

We used to think there was one kind of chimpanzee, living in the dense forests of west and central Africa. Then a few years ago came reports of a slightly smaller race or subspecies in a wet and tropical stretch of forest in east central DR Congo, between the Zaire (Congo) and Lualaba Rivers. Eventually scientists decided that this was a separate species, which they called pygmy chimpanzee, and native Africans call "bonobo" (see page 12 for Fact File).

Both kinds of chimpanzees have thin, shiny, dark brown or black fur. Young ones have a prominent white patch on the lower back, which they lose as they grow older. Their faces are bare, showing different expressions like human smiles and frowns. In common chimpanzees, males grow slightly larger and heavier than females. In pygmy chimpanzees the sexes are similar, and the largest is only as big as a well-grown female common chimpanzee. The most striking difference is in the faces. As they grow older, common chimpanzees develop a longer jaw and heavier brow ridges. Pygmy chimpanzees keep a round, young-looking face throughout life.

You SELDOM SEE ONE CHIMPANZEE of either species on its own. Usually they live together in small bands, perhaps two or three mothers with young, accompanying one old male and two or three younger ones. Chimpanzees in a band behave as a family. The old male is the father figure, dominating the others, threatening and leading attacks on other bands that move too close. He takes the lead in moving from one area to another, in a constant search for ripe fruits and new shoots. Younger males give way to the older ones, learning from them and taking over leadership as they mature.

Within the families they keep close to each other, grooming each other's fur, removing twigs and parasites. Older ones play with the young, sometimes threatening, sometimes smacking or biting

gently if they misbehave. Young chimpanzees are light enough to climb readily and swing from tree branches. Older ones become too heavy, and tend to stay on the ground, climbing only to find fruit and to make a nest for sleeping at night.

Using a stick to dig out termites

Two adult chimps with their young

Where food is plentiful locally, several bands come together, forming groups of 30 or 40. When the food becomes scarce, the bands quarrel among themselves and go their separate ways to search for more. While much of their food lies in the forests, chimpanzees sometimes come into conflict with farmers, whose plantations and farms bear rich crops of figs, bananas and other fruit in season.

Family group of chimps sitting in a tree

A helping hand from mother

FAMILY LIFE

Chimpanzees are mainly vegetarian, eating leaves, shoots, flowers and fruit that they pull from trees and shrubs, and roots dug from the soft earth. In the rain forest, different species of trees flower and produce their fruits at different times of the year, so the bands are traveling constantly. Younger males learn from the older ones where food is to be found in different seasons. Chimpanzees also search bark and fallen logs for insects, and break into nests of termites and bees, using sticks and stones as tools. They take birds' eggs and chicks, and small mammals, including monkeys.

They breed throughout the year. When a female becomes sexually attractive, she gives off a scent that may attract other males to the band. The band leader is the one most likely to mate with her, but younger males may be successful too. She bears a single young about eight months later. The baby holds on to the mother's fur, at first drinking milk from her breasts. Then, clinging to her shoulder, it learns to share the different kinds of food that she eats herself. Mothers and young stay together for two or three years, sometimes longer.

Where do they live?

Common chimpanzees live in the dense rain forests of tropical Africa, from Senegal in the west through Nigeria, Cameroon, Gabon and DR Congo to Uganda and Tanzania in the east. Formerly plentiful, they are now becoming much rarer because of hunting and local destruction of the forest for timber and agriculture. Pygmy chimpanzees have a more restricted range in the equatorial forests of eastern DR Congo. We do not know how many there are, but they are also likely to be at risk as human populations expand (see page 42).

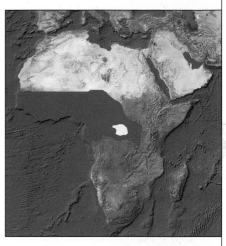

■ Common chimpanzees
□ Pygmy chimpanzees

HOW HUMAN?

Scientists tell us that chimpanzees differ from us only slightly—less than any other ape—in genetic makeup. It is not surprising, therefore, that chimpanzees can be trained to sit on chairs for a zoo tea party, pour tea from a teapot and throw buns around, making them act more or less like ill-behaved children. For television commercials they can be trained to wear suits, dresses and bonnets. With human voices added, they can be made to look human enough to be living next door.

However, this training hides some important features that make chimpanzees very different from humans. Their limbs, for example, are proportionately longer than ours. They walk on all fours as much as on two legs, and their big toes, like their thumbs, can be used for gripping. Though more clumsy than we are at walking and running, they are stronger for their weight, and young ones are better at climbing and moving through trees. They are almost completely covered with body hair, except for their faces, which are mobile and expressive like our own.

One important similarity is their ability to make and use tools. They can make a digging stick, for example, by stripping leaves off a branch, and they can join sticks together to use as a lever. To threaten they can wave clubs or bang them on the ground. They can throw branches or stones, though not very accurately, at enemies or predators.

An important difference is their use of sound. They have many different calls, from screams to muttering, which express their feelings or needs. But they have never developed use of words to express ideas. For important similarities and differences in brain structure, and other aspects of behavior, see pages 40–41.

GREAT APES: GORILLAS

The largest living apes, found in mountain and lowland forests of Africa.

FACT FILE

Suborder:	Anthropoidea
Family:	Pongidae
Scientific name:	*Gorilla gorilla*
Color:	Dark brown to blue-black
Weight:	Males 350 lb (160 kg), females 200 lb (90 kg)
Length, head and body:	Males 5 ft 7 in (1.7 m), females 4 ft 11 in (1.5 m)
Habitat:	Tropical lowland and mountain forest
Range:	Central Africa

Lowland gorilla baby, 2 months old

RELATIONSHIPS

There are three quite separate stocks of gorillas, generally similar in appearance but different enough in detail to be called subspecies:

- Western lowland gorilla, *Gorilla gorilla gorilla*
- Eastern lowland gorilla, *Gorilla gorilla graueri*
- Mountain gorilla *Gorilla gorilla beringei.*

Eastern gorillas tend to be darker than western, with heavier jaws and brow ridges. Mountain gorillas have shorter arms and longer fur. Though formerly these stocks must have intermingled, they are now geographically isolated, with little or no contact between them in the wild.

LIFE OF GORILLAS

Gorillas share with orangutans the longest gestation periods of all the big apes. Their babies are born some 36 or 37 weeks after a successful mating—about two weeks shorter than in humans. Gorilla babies feed on their mothers' milk for at least three years, then the young take a further nine or ten years to reach adult size and sexual maturity. They may live a further 25–30 years.

GORILLAS MOVE THROUGH the undergrowth in bands, usually of up to a dozen, but sometimes as many as 30. You always know when they are around. Largest of the apes, much larger than most other animals that share their forests, they have little to fear and nothing to hide. When a band is near, you hear them pushing through the undergrowth, grunting quietly to each other, occasionally barking or beating their chests with a hollow sound. If one sees you, it roars to let others know there is an intruder.

The dominant male of the party, huge and silver-backed, and some of the younger males may threaten with more chest-beating and roaring. They may charge, which usually means that you have approached too suddenly, and startled them. However, gorillas are peace-loving animals, more likely to disappear quietly into the forest than to waste energy in chasing strangers.

Other signs of their presence are crudely built nests of leaves and stalks, on the ground or in low bushes, where they have slept overnight, and patches of vegetation, some eaten, the rest trampled and rolled over. Wherever they go, gorillas leave a persistent musky scent, which may warn other bands of their presence.

FAMILY LIFE

Wandering in bands through the forest, gorillas feed almost entirely on leaves, shoots and roots, and occasionally on fruit, which they pluck and manipulate with their hands. The front teeth are sharp-edged for biting, the back teeth flattened and smoothed for grinding vegetation. Because leaves and shoots have little nourishment and are hard to digest, they have to eat huge amounts to obtain the energy they need. This may be one reason for their large size.

They breed throughout the year. A female may come on heat in any month. She mates with one or several males within the group, and gives birth to a single baby some 36 or 37 weeks later. Weighing about 5 lb (2.3 kg) at birth, the baby holds tightly to the mother's silky fur, traveling wherever she goes, and growing quickly on her milk. After three to four months a baby can roll and play with others of the band, and be tended and guarded by other mothers as well as its own.

Young gorilla swinging; older ones grow too fat and heavy

Mountain gorilla family group

Where do they live?

Western lowland gorillas live in the rain forests of Cameroon, Gabon, Congo and Nigeria, west of the Congo (Zaire) River, on the coastal plains and mountains up to about 6,000 ft (1,800 m). Eastern lowland gorillas live in forests of eastern DR Congo, between the Lualaba River and the Great Rift Valley, at heights of up to about 8,000 ft (2,400 m). Mountain gorillas live in highland forests that grow on a range of volcanic peaks north and west of Lake Kivu, on the borderland of DR Congo, Uganda and Rwanda. This is a cloudy, damp and often cold environment, at heights of 9,000–12,000 ft (2,700–3,700 m). Their slightly longer and denser fur may help them to keep warm on chilly mornings.

- ■ Western lowland gorilla
- □ Eastern lowland gorilla
- ▦ Mountain gorilla

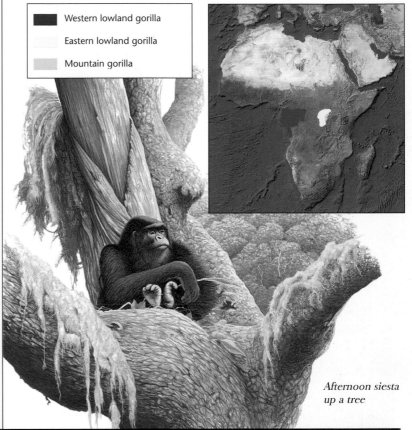

Afternoon siesta up a tree

WHERE HAVE THEY GONE?

Within the equatorial forest, gorillas were almost certainly more plentiful and widespread in the past. The explorers who first identified them were horrified. They seemed like huge, fierce hairy people, much larger and more threatening than the native Africans, and much to be feared. Though gorillas are in fact gentle animals, and very unlikely to attack humans, many were shot on sight.

We do not know how many gorillas are left in the world today because they are difficult to count. Recent estimates suggest about 100,000 in the western lowlands, between 5,000 and 10,000 in the eastern lowlands, and perhaps fewer than 600 in the mountains. Why so few? Mostly because huge areas of forest have been cut down for timber or cleared for farming. Soon there will be still fewer gorillas, because the destruction continues. Destroying the gorillas' home is the surest way to destroy gorillas (see pages 42–43).

Lowland gorilla

THE HUMAN FAMILY

Ground-living primates that have reached the top of the tree.

FACT FILE

MODERN HUMAN

Suborder:	Anthropoidea
Family:	Hominidae
Scientific name:	*Homo sapiens*
Color:	Variable, pink to black; head and (male) face furry, sparse body fur, usually clothed
Weight:	Males 160 lb (73 kg), females 140 lb (64 kg)
Height:	Males 5 ft 11 in (1.8 m), females 5 ft 3 in (1.6 m)
Habitat:	All habitats, tropical to polar
Range:	Worldwide

RELATIONSHIPS

What is our relationship to the monkeys and apes that we match most closely? This is the subject of a big argument, involving both biologists and nonbiologists. "Evolutionists" believe that we evolved (developed) from ground-living apelike ancestors. "Creationists" believe that we came into being much as we are today (see opposite page).

WHAT IMPORTANT DIFFERENCES set humans apart from apes and other animals?

- *Upright stance.* Apes need support when standing upright. With a different shape of pelvis, "S"-curved spine, and angled skull, humans stand upright normally and easily.
- *Walking.* Apes when walking support their upper body on their long arms, touching the ground with their knuckles. Humans walk upright, rolling on the feet from toes to heel, leaving hands and arms free for other activities.
- *Diet, jaws and teeth.* Apes need large teeth and jaws, both for grinding vegetable food and for fighting. Eating a mixed diet, and fighting with hands and weapons, humans get by with much smaller jaws, teeth and facial muscles.

- *Brain size.* The largest apes have brains of up to about 35 in³ (600 cm³) in volume. Early humans of similar body size had brains approaching twice that volume, and modern man has brains of 90–120 in³ (1,500–2,000 cm³). Much of the extra brain gives humans more efficient memories and ways of thinking.
- *Language.* Apes express simple ideas with calls and grunts. They can be trained to recognize human words, but cannot speak them and have no equivalent words of their own. We think and express thoughts in strings of words, called language, and can record them in different ways to pass from one generation to the next.

Where did they live?

The earliest near-human fossil remains appear in Olduvai Gorge, east Africa, and are about 1.75 million years old. Though given the name *Homo habilis*, meaning "skillful man," they are now thought to represent small, semi-upright apes, with brain capacity 40 in³ (700 cm³), which lived in a dry, warm climate, and hunted in grassland and along the forest edge.

The earliest remains that are generally agreed to be human have been found at several sites, including central Java, China, Africa and Europe. Though all were given separate names when discovered, they are now bundled together as *Homo erectus* ("upright man"). Dating from about 1 million to 300,000 years ago, they represent a small kind of human with brain capacity of 50–60 in³ (900–1,000 cm³), who hunted, and used simple tools and fire.

Homo sapiens ("wise man"), our own species, appears first in fossil deposits about 250,000 years old. These too are widespread, and vary in size and proportions between sites. Skulls and other bones dating from about 40,000 years ago are indistinguishable from those of modern humans. *Homo sapiens* also spread across Africa, Europe and Asia, and was the only human species to spread to North and South America, crossing the Bering Bridge (then dry land, now the Bering Strait) about 12,000 years ago.

Though originally a species of warm grassland and forest edge, humans have adapted to every climate and habitat from the hottest, wettest tropical forests to some of the driest deserts.

African bushman of today

HUMAN POPULATION GROWTH

For many thousands of years the human population remained small. While we lived in small groups, hunting and gathering our food like other primates, there were probably just a few hundred thousand of us worldwide. Then we began to grow food instead of hunt for it, live in villages instead of wandering bands, manufacture goods and trade with each other, and our population began expanding.

Now there are 6 billion of us, and we have come to dominate the world.

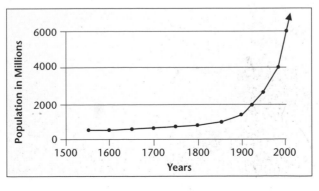

THE EVOLUTIONIST WAY

Evolutionary biologists believe that all the different kinds of animals, such as penguins, tigers and bears, evolved naturally from earlier forms, called "common ancestors," that were similar but not exactly the same. How did this come about? "Natural variations," the slight differences between individuals of a species, were acted on by "natural selection," so that animals that varied in ways that best fitted their environment survived and bred, while those that varied in less-fitting ways died out.

Evolutionists regard humans as part of this process—simply another kind of ape, which evolved from ground-living apes similar to chimpanzees.

THE CREATIONIST WAY

Creationists, whether biologists or nonbiologists, believe that evolution by natural selection could never have brought about the big differences between penguins, tigers and bears, nor could monkeys, apes and humans have evolved from earlier common ancestors. They believe instead that these different forms came into existence more or less as we know them today—they were "created," rather than evolving.

However, creationists differ in their views on how the creations came about. Some see creation as a natural process, though a different one from the evolutionary process. Others take literally the words of the Book of Genesis, Chapter 1, in the Bible: God created the great whales, the winged fowl, the cattle, and finally created man in His own image.

Here we do not take sides in the argument about human origins. You may want to follow it up one day, and decide on what you think is right. We are interested only in the similarities and differences between humans and the rest of the animal world.

- *Tool making and using.* Monkeys use stones or twigs as tools. Apes may shorten twigs to make them more efficient for particular purposes. Humans make and use tools all the time, from spades to bulldozers, from scooters to intercontinental aircraft, for different purposes.
- *Growing up.* Young apes take 10–12 years to become adults. Human children can breed from about 12 years, but do not stop growing until they are 18–20, and may then spend several more years learning culture in school or college.
- *Communities.* Monkeys and apes live in bands that keep together by sight, hearing and touch. Language and technology enable humans to live in much bigger groups, from villages to cities of several million inhabitants.
- *Other differences.* Can you think of other ways in which humans differ from other animals?

MONKEYS AND APES AT RISK

Which are the endangered species?

ENDANGERING OTHER ANIMALS

Of the countless different species of animals that have lived on earth, hundreds of thousands no longer exist. They have become extinct. Yet new species have constantly appeared to take their places.

Most of these extinctions happened before man came on the scene. Some are happening now. There are species alive today that will disappear within the next 40–50 years, either through

Endangered mountain gorilla

natural causes, or because humans are helping to destroy them.

When our ancestors first appeared on earth, and for a long time after, they were no more important than dozens of other kinds of medium to large mammals that lived at the same time. They hunted the plains and gathered food, as some monkeys and apes do today, breeding at about the same rate, living and dying much as they do.

Then gradually their ways of life changed. Perhaps their big brains and intelligence made them too successful as hunters. Certainly over tens of thousands of years they wiped out whole stocks of other mammals across Asia and Europe.

Our ancestors developed tools and skills for clearing the forests, tilling the land, raising crops and domesticating animals. They dug deep for fuel and valuable minerals, and learned to deal with injury and illness, to avoid starvation and to destroy predators. More of their babies survived and lived longer.

The result was an enormous increase in human population, from tens of thousands to millions, and then to billions. Human population continues to increase, every day demanding more and more land and resources, and edging other animals out of their homes.

M AN CAN DESTROY STOCKS of monkeys and apes in many ways, sometimes willfully, sometimes almost without trying.

■ *Hunting for food.* Villagers in many forested areas catch and kill monkeys for food. Where monkeys are plentiful, where there is plenty of forest for them to hide in, and where the villagers have other sources of food, this is not very important.
■ *Hunting for pets.* This can be more damaging, particularly to stocks of such attractive species as marmosets and tamarins, which may already be at risk.
■ *Hunting for sale to suppliers and traders.* This can be very damaging. The demand may be great and, because so many die in captivity,

more monkeys and apes are taken than are actually needed.
■ *Forest clearance.* Every patch of forest cleared displaces native animals. If many areas are cut, surviving animals have fewer places for refuge. Forest clearance is the main reason why so many stocks of monkeys and apes are currently at risk.

Thus the most serious causes of danger are trading and forest clearance. The best ways to protect the monkeys and apes are: (1) To discover as exactly as possible their numbers and needs. (2) To prohibit all trading except under license, and to issue licenses only for species or stocks known to be plentiful. (3) To ensure that forestry, too, is allowed only under license, and that large blocks of forest remain as reserves for the native animals.

Golden lion tamarin

Mountain gorilla

MONKEYS AND APES AT RISK

Which kinds of monkeys and apes are currently at risk? IUCN, an international conservation organization with headquarters in Switzerland, estimates that almost half the living species of monkeys and apes are endangered in one way or another. Here are just a few of them:

1. Golden lion tamarin, *Leontopithecus rosalia.* These beautiful little animals live in small remnants of forest in the hills north of Rio de Janeiro, southeastern Brazil. They are pretty enough to be much in demand as pets, and forest clearance, due to pressures of human population, has left them with very little living space. There may be only a few dozen remaining in the wild.

2. Lion-tailed macaque, *Macaca silenus.* This shaggy black macaque, with a strikingly handsome gray mane and beard, lives in dense forests of the Western Ghats, a mountain range in southwest India. Named for the tuft of fur on its long tail, it is seldom seen these days, and may have been hunted almost to destruction.

3. Golden snub-nosed monkey, *Rhinopithecus roxellana.* Snub-nosed monkeys form one of the branches of the colobus monkey group (pages 26–27), distinguished by thick lips and curiously upturned nostrils. They live in mountain forests of eastern China and Vietnam. This species, the golden snub-nosed, has thick brown fur laced with gold, yellow-gold feet and bright blue eye rings. Much in demand as pets, they are becoming extremely rare in the wild.

4. Yellow-tailed woolly monkey, *Lagothrix flavicauda.* This is a big New World monkey of the cebid family (pages 18–19) that lives in damp, tropical forests of the Peruvian Andes. The name comes from a yellow stripe on the long, prehensile tail. The fur, reddish brown, is dense and velvety, and much valued by local people to decorate clothing.

5. Silvery gibbon, *Hylobates moloch.* Gibbons (pages 30–31) live almost entirely in trees. They get to know their way around their own patch of forest, and are totally lost when the chain saws move in. This is a species whose forests on the island of Java are gradually being cut down for their valuable timber. There are probably only a few hundred of them left.

6. Sumatran orangutan, *Pongo pygmaeus abelii.* We have met these endearing apes before (pages 34–35). Not only is their forest being systematically destroyed for timber, but they are also popular as household pets—at least until they grow big enough to become a nuisance. So their numbers are declining steadily—there is an estimated 5,000–7,000 of them left.

7. Mountain gorilla, *Gorilla gorilla beringei.* The damp, overgrown forested slopes of central Africa have long been the home of these huge, gentle animals. They are shy and need plenty of space. Few remain, as gradually their forests are being taken over for agriculture.

Golden snub-nosed monkey

HOW CAN WE HELP?

- Join a national or international conservation group dedicated to protecting and conserving wildlife, especially monkeys and apes. There are several addresses on page 45.
- Help the group to raise money for research on monkeys and apes, and to support schemes for their protection.
- Learn all you can about monkeys and apes. Read about them, watch TV programs, videos and films, and tell all your friends about them. Get as many people as you can to support their protection and conservation.
- Visit parks and reserves where monkeys and apes live. Ask the park managers, rangers or guides what species are present and how they are faring.
- Visit zoos to see how well their monkeys and apes are kept, and talk to the keepers and managers about them. Are they lively and well fed? Have they plenty of room? Are they breeding? If you feel they are badly looked after, complain first to the manager, then to the city or town council that licenses the zoo and allows it to stay open.
- Remember that, where monkeys and apes live close to people, the people may be very poor. They will be tempted to kill animals that destroy their crops, or trade in them for money. Support organizations that help people, monkeys and apes to live alongside each other.
- If you live in a country that has wild monkeys and apes, encourage your national and local governments and your local community to support wildlife of all kinds, including their monkeys and apes.
- Visit national parks and reserves where monkeys and apes live, and encourage others to do the same.

Sumatran orangutan

GLOSSARY

Can you identify the species pictured?
(answers below)

adaptation	Change in a plant or animal that increases the chance of survival
aggression	Readiness to attack
ancestors	Parents, grandparents and earlier generations
Bering Bridge	Dry land between northern Asia and North America, which existed when sea level was lower
brachiation	Swinging through the trees using arms, legs, and sometimes the tail
canine teeth	Usually the longest, sharpest teeth, at the front corner of each jaw
canopy	Treetops
carnivore	Animal that feeds mainly on the flesh of other animals
conservation	Saving and protecting species, usually by protecting the places where they live
density	Number (of animals or plants) in a particular area
digestive system	Parts of an animal in which food is broken down and absorbed (mouth, throat, stomach, intestines and so on)
dominant	Most important, able to control others
forage	To search for food
fossil	Remnant of ancient plant or animal preserved in stone
genus	Group of closely related animals or plants (plural, "genera")
gestation period	Length of time it takes for baby animals to grow inside their mother
habitat	Place where a plant or animal lives
herbivore	Animal that feeds mainly on vegetation (plant life)
litter	Group of young animals that are born and raised together
mane	Long hair on the neck and shoulders
molar teeth	Teeth at the back of the mouth, used for grinding food
monitoring	Watching carefully to see what progress is being made
New World	North and South America (see Old World)
nocturnal	At night, describing animals that hunt or forage by night
Old World	Europe and Asia (see New World)
omnivorous	Eating both animal and vegetable foods

From top: lemur, douroucouli, colobus, orangutan

paleontologist	Scientist who studies bones and other fossil remains
poachers	Illegal hunters
population	Part of a species living in a particular area, sometimes but not always separated geographically from other populations of the same species (see **stock**)
predator	Animal that hunts, kills and eats other animals
pregnant	Carrying a developing baby or babies inside the body
prehensile tail	A tail the tip of which can curl around and grasp a branch
prosimians	Monkeylike animals such as lemurs and lorises
rodents	Mammals with sharp, chisel-like front teeth, such as mice, rats and squirrels
savannah	Grassland with trees and shrubs
scavenge	Eat rubbish or old food that has been lying around for some time
simian	Monkeylike
species	A particular kind of plant or animal
stock	Small group of animals or plants of one species, forming part of a population (see **population**)

Useful addresses

International Primate Protection League,
116 Judd Street, London WC1H 9NS
(Tel: 020 7837 7227)

International Primate Protection League,
PO Box 766, Summerville, SC 29484, USA

Monkey World, Longthorns, East Stoke,
Wareham, Dorset DH20 6HH
(Tel: 01929 462537)

Orangutan Foundation, 7 Kent Terrace,
London NW1 4RP (Tel: 020 7724 2912)

Orangutan Foundation International,
822 South Wellesley Avenue,
Los Angeles CA 90049 Tel: (310)207 1655)

Durrell Wildlife Conservation Trust, Trinity,
Jersey, Channel Islands JE3 5BP
(Tel: 01534 860000)

WWF (UK), Panda House, Weyside Park,
Cattershall Lane, Godalming,
Surrey GU7 1XR
(Tel: 01483 426 444; Fax: 01483 426 409)

WWF (USA), 1250 24th St NW, Suite 500,
Washington DC 20037

WWF (Australia), Level 5, 725 George St,
Sydney, NSW 2000

WWF (South Africa), 116 Dorp Street,
Stellenbosch 7600

From top: Barbary macaque, red uakari, tarsier, pileated gibbon

INDEX